BONE BROTH MIRACLE™
DIET
INSTANT POT
COOKBOOK

T0070976

BONE BROTH MIRACLE™
DIET
INSTANT POT
COOKBOOK

AN ANCIENT HEALTH & BEAUTY REMEDY
MADE EASY & DELICIOUS

Johanna Reagan

Skyhorse Publishing

Copyright © 2020 by Hollan Publishing, Inc.

All rights reserved. No part of this book may be reproduced in any manner without the express written consent of the publisher, except in the case of brief excerpts in critical reviews or articles.

All inquiries should be addressed to Skyhorse Publishing, 307 West 36th Street, 11th Floor, New York, NY 10018.

Skyhorse Publishing books may be purchased in bulk at special discounts for sales promotion, corporate gifts, fund-raising, or educational purposes. Special editions can also be created to specifications. For details, contact the Special Sales Department, Skyhorse Publishing, 307 West 36th Street, 11th Floor, New York, NY 10018 or info@skyhorsepublishing.com.

Skyhorse® and Skyhorse Publishing® are registered trademarks of Skyhorse Publishing, Inc.®, a Delaware corporation.

Visit our website at www.skyhorsepublishing.com.

10 9 8 7 6 5 4 3 2 1

Library of Congress Cataloging-in-Publication Data is available on file.

Cover design by Daniel Brount
Images used under license from Shutterstock.com

Print ISBN: 978-1-5107-5166-8
Ebook ISBN: 978-1-5107-5167-5

Printed in China

table of contents

Introducing . . . Bone Broth in an Instant

Some things are just meant to be together: cookies and milk, salt and pepper, spaghetti and meatballs. And while it may not roll off the tongue quite so easily, this cookbook humbly presents two items that are perfectly paired in the kitchen: homemade bone broth and an Instant Pot.

Bone broth is a nutrient-dense superfood made from meat bones. It's soothing and easy on the digestion, with a ton of health benefits to drink in. (More on that in a bit.) An Instant Pot is a brand-name pressure cooker that gives new meaning to the term "set it and forget it." Forget needing to constantly monitor a simmering pot of bone broth for up to 24 hours! Although that has traditionally been the best way to make bone broth, it's not usually a very realistic option. That's where the Instant Pot swoops in and saves the day. It creates perfect bone broths in *only 2 hours* . . . with no stirring or monitoring necessary. Press a few buttons and let the Instant Pot take over from there. And with that broth you made so easily, you can then make hundreds of classic and new soups, chilis, stews, drinks, and main dishes using the Instant Pot. Ready to put the power of the Pot and ingenious bone broth recipes to work for you? *Bone Broth Miracle Diet Instant Pot Cookbook* has just what you need!

- Part 1: Bone Broth Made Easy & Delicious dives into bone broth, its history, its health benefits, and tricks and tips for making great broth every time. You'll also discover why the Instant Pot is such an essential tool in the bone broth–making process.
- Part 2: Recipes for Flavor & Health offers more than 80 ways to make bone broth and use your homemade broth to create

delicious dishes the whole family will love. From basic bone broths to get you started to drinks and tonics made with bone broth to savor and boost your health, there are so many ideas to include bone broth in your daily menu. You'll taste how bone broth works so well in soups, stews, and chilis. But don't stop there! Any recipe that traditionally uses broth or even plain water can benefit from the addition of bone broth. You'll learn how in the Main Events section—and get some ideas for bringing bone broth into favorite recipes from your own collection.

Now, let's get out the Instant Pot and cook up something good!

PART 1

Bone Broth Made Easy & Delicious

What Is Bone Broth?

Bone broth is so simple and so good. What we recognize as bone broth today begins from a combination of marrow-filled and cartilage-packed bones (from your choice of chicken, beef, turkey, lamb, pork, or even fish), mixed vegetables, water, and a splash of vinegar or citrus. The result is amazingly flavorful and beneficial for your health. But bone broth's use as a soothing cup or bowl of healing is not really new. It's commonly believed that for as long as humans have been hunting animals for their meat, we have been boiling their bones too.

Long History of Healing

Soup may very well be the first example of human cuisine. Heatproof containers perfect for boiling water were invented somewhere between five thousand and nine thousand years ago, but it is possible that cooking broth may go back even further. The recent discovery of heatproof pottery in Xianrendong Cave in China suggests that bowls for cooking and eating were used as early as twenty thousand years ago. Keep in mind that many archaeologists have pointed out that pottery was not even needed for preparing meals, as long as a ditch lined with animal skins and fire-heated rocks were available. So pinpointing the very first introduction of soup or broth would be difficult. Whatever the time span, it is widely agreed that the leftover broth from boiling meat and bones was a large part of early diets.

Historians also know that bone broth was valued for more than everyday sustenance and energy. Physicians as far back as Hippocrates proclaimed its many health benefits, and nearly every early civilization had its own versions of bone broth. In the twelfth century, the Jewish physician Moses Maimonides wrote extensively on the therapeutic qualities of chicken soup. In his work *Medical Responsa*, Maimonides recommended chicken broth to "neutralize body constitution" and also cure asthma and leprosy. While the leprosy claim didn't pan out, the key ingredients in chicken broth were ultimately shown to be anti-inflammatory and assist with cold-related respiratory problems in a 2000 study by researchers at the University of Nebraska Medical Center in Omaha.

Bringing Back the Broth

Somewhere in our "evolution," we lost widespread appreciation for simple healing from the kitchen. Thankfully, this age-old culinary staple is now being rediscovered and savored beyond just an ingredient used to make soups. Bone broth's benefits are becoming

more widely publicized and accepted, and it now stands on its own as an invigorating health drink or as an addition to family-favorite recipes to boost nutrition and rich taste. So why isn't this superfood part of our meals every day?

Until recently, there has still been one major barrier to bone broth's use in most households' kitchens. Traditionally, bone broth's ingredients have often been cooked over the course of a day or, at the least, many hours—the best way known to infuse minerals, vitamins, and amino acids from gelatin in the bones into the resulting broth. The combination of nourishing elements and the flavor released in the long cooking process makes bone broth not only good for you but also richly appetizing. But the lengthy cooking method has deterred many from taking full advantage of bone broth's culinary magic and healing powers in our busy modern lives. That's why introducing the Instant Pot as a way to cook bone broth is such a game changer! It delivers all the benefits through a method that produces results just as delicious and nutritious as hours of simmering.

The Power in Bone Broth

Think of the soothing and healing simple broth brings when someone has a cold or stomach flu. Just sipping on pure broth suddenly brings renewed energy to body and spirit. So it shouldn't be a surprise how powerful bone broth can be for health. When we take a look at its nutritional profile, it's even more obvious that if you're missing out on bone broth, you're missing out on a simple way to nurture your body. That's an important realization at a time when health really needs a boost.

Although we are becoming more advanced in many areas such as technology and transportation, our health is deteriorating. While we are much less likely than previous generations to die of infectious disease, we are now significantly *more* likely to experience chronic disease.

The Difference Diet Can Make

The real problem here is that modern diets look nothing like those that humans consumed for the vast majority of our existence. Thus, there is a mismatch between what we eat and what our bodies are designed to digest. The problem is somewhat like putting diesel fuel in a car designed for unleaded. Just as that car wouldn't make it far down the road, modern humans are experiencing breakdowns in health. Despite medical advances, the life expectancy of some demographics of "Westerners" is decreasing for the first time since governments started keeping records. Western societies are actually experiencing *increasing* incidences of the following diet-related chronic diseases and conditions:

- Obesity
- Cardiovascular disease
- Cancer

- Autoimmune diseases (such as celiac, rheumatoid arthritis, type 1 diabetes, Hashimoto's thyroiditis, lupus, and inflammatory bowel disease)
- Type 2 diabetes
- Asthma
- Depression and anxiety
- ADHD
- Autism
- Osteoporosis

So, Now What?

When we try to wade through which foods make smart choices, it is essential to consider whether a food was historically a part of our diets or whether it is a new introduction. Many diet and health experts value this back-to-basics approach and point to the overwhelming portion of our diet made up of wheat, soy, corn, and refined sugar. Our current diet is completely unlike anything our species has encountered before. No wonder we are experiencing a meltdown of modern health!

In fact, we can see this phenomenon in real time. As Western-style diets become more popular across the globe, each new nation that adopts them predictably begins to experience increased rates of these modern diseases. Only by going back to traditional diets can we regain our wellness. The reintroduction of bone broth is an important part of that transition. Bone broth was an effective, efficient staple of our hunter-gatherer ancestors for centuries. It provides a savory "umami" flavor and incredible health benefits.

Gifts in the Pot

Broth has so much to offer our health and nutrition. Unfortunately, it has not been well researched, simply because it's a food that can't be patented; the research dollars that go into pharmaceuticals just aren't there. Additionally, creating identical batches of broth that satisfy scientific rigor is nearly impossible, and this further complicates the issue. However, there is good evidence for the benefits of the compounds *within* bone broth.

Collagen and Gelatin

There is more to healthy and strong bones than just eating or drinking your daily dose of calcium. Collagen is found almost everywhere in the body, but primarily in bones and connective tissues. Historically, people have boiled down the collagen-rich bones, skin, and tissue of animals for hearty cooking, but also to transform the collagen into gelatin for glue. Collagen and gelatin are crucial factors in maintaining bone, cartilage, joint, and intestinal health, and are far and away the most healthful elements of bone broth. Collagen helps build sturdy bodies, strong joints, healthy organs, and beautiful skin. Without it, muscles can weaken, bones become brittle, and skin loses its elasticity—or in other words, becomes wrinkly. As we age, we see the effects of diminishing collagen from the wear and tear in our bones and joints to the sagging bags underneath our eyes.

Gelatin is the source we use to replenish the collagen in our body, and it is made up of 84 to 90 percent protein. While collagen is a protein coming directly from the body, gelatin is a food product made by denaturing—or cooking—foods that contain collagen. This process is something that we do regularly when cooking meals but rarely think about in that way; by roasting, boiling, grilling, braising, or otherwise cooking meat that contains collagen-rich bones, skin, and connective tissue, natural gelatin is being added to our food.

Amino Acids

The benefits of gelatin in food have a lot to do with the amino acids released in its production. Namely, nonessential amino acids such as glycine, glutamine, proline, and alanine are present in gelatin and can do wonders for the body. They are called "nonessential" because, technically, the body is capable of producing them on its own. However, when the body is stressed, healing from injury, or funneling out other toxins, it may not be able to keep up with the demand. It is important to eat foods rich in collagen so that the body is never deprived of these reparative resources.

Glycine, glutamine, proline, and alanine are the four most prevalent amino acids in collagen and are vital resources that bodies in times of stress so desperately need. Let's look more closely at each one.

Glycine

Glycine is a building block of protein. It is the smallest of the amino acid structures. Glycine participates in the production of muscle tissue and conversion of glucose into energy. It is also found in the skin and connective tissues and makes up nearly one-third of the collagen structure. For its wound-healing properties, glycine has been used in topical creams for skin ulcers and other skin abrasions.

The body can produce glycine with other existing chemicals in healthy individuals. Even for the healthiest of people, however, periodic illness, infection, or pregnancy can strain the naturally occurring levels of glycine. For those suffering from chronic ailments such as inflammation, the body may not be able to make up the necessary glycine to support healthy function.

As a glucogenic amino acid, glycine assists in regulating blood sugar levels, energy levels, DNA and RNA, and the production of bile in the stomach in order to digest fats. It is often used as an ingredient in store-bought antacids for this reason and is recommended by doctors to aid in gastrointestinal disorders and acid reflux. It has been used in treating symptoms of hypoglycemia, chronic fatigue syndrome, anemia, and other problems associated with low energy in the body.

Glycine is also useful in the body's detoxification process. The liver is the body's natural filter of toxins—from alcohol, narcotics, and prescription drugs to preservatives, chemicals, and other impurities in the blood coming from the digestive tract. Small amounts of glycine have been shown to provide protective benefits for the liver, particularly in response to the harmful effects of alcohol.

Maintaining a healthy diet with foods that contain collagen—including bone broth—can help strengthen the body's supply of glycine. Glycine is also found in foods high in protein, such as legumes, dairy, fish, and meat products. Incorporating these foods into your diet on a regular basis helps ensure that the body has the strengthening amino acids that it needs to thrive.

Glutamine

Another nonessential amino acid, glutamine, or glutamic acid, assists the body in gut health and immunity and is primarily made and found in the body's muscles. The blood distributes glutamine throughout the body, directing it to the places that need it most. It stimulates immune cells and is crucial in cell proliferation in muscles, which benefits all sorts of healing processes for burns, trauma, injuries, illnesses, stress, and even the regrowth of villi in the small intestines. Intestinal villi are small strands that project from the intestinal wall and make it easier for the intestines to absorb nutrients during digestion. For individuals whose villi have been compromised by gut disorders, such as Crohn's disease, celiac sprue, and ulcers, the restorative power of glutamine is even more important.

Glutamine can also be helpful for weight problems, both in terms of excessive weight and underweight. Doctors and nutritionists have always recommended nutrient-rich soups as a part of a healthier diet and for calorie control, but the glutamine in bone broth is restorative for muscle proteins and helps prevent atrophy, which is when the muscles deteriorate due to malnourishment or lack of use. Atrophy occurs when the body is overworked and is using up more glutamine than the muscles can reasonably replenish. In addition, the glutamine in soups helps curb cravings for carbohydrates and sugar, which are arguably the two most problematic modern food addictions. This boost in metabolism helps maintain healthy muscles and is an essential part of the nourishing effects of bone broth.

Proline

Proline is a fundamental part of collagen and cartilage production. It is prevalent in animal protein, and therefore it is unlikely that individuals who consume healthy, omnivorous diets will ever suffer from insufficient amounts of proline. For many Americans, however, high-carbohydrate, low-fat, and low-protein diets are the norm, which can become problematic for proline production and maintaining healthy skin and connective tissue. As we now know, proline is abundant in bone broth.

Alanine

Alanine supports liver function, glucose production, and the citric acid cycle, which merges fat, protein, and carbohydrate production. This nonessential amino acid is the supplement of choice for many athletes. While the body makes alanine independently, additional doses of it create the potential to build greater muscle mass and increase endurance. Although many people associate this supplement with bodybuilders, it can also be beneficial to the elderly who have weakened muscles and strained physical movement.

Although glycine, glutamine, proline, glycine, and alanine are nonessential amino acids, this does not mean there is an everlasting supply. Their nourishing effects can be added to anyone's diet simply by drinking or using bone broth in cooking. Healthy diets filled with animal protein and nourishing vegetables

help support the production of these amino acids and the role they play in building and maintaining collagen in the body. In the American diet, more people choose to eat boneless meats like chicken or turkey breast in order to avoid fat and for easier preparation and handling. As a result, the parts of the animal that are dense in collagen are tossed away, as are all of the great benefits of their consumption. Unless this cultural tendency toward only eating muscle meats shifts to include more bone meats, adding bone broth to everyone's regular diet can counteract this problem.

Vitamins and Minerals

Among the many health benefits of bone broth is the mineral content of this nourishing liquid. Minerals such as calcium, magnesium, phosphorous, and potassium are released as the bones soften and break down in the heat when making broth. While the precise amounts of vitamins and minerals in each batch of broth can differ, you'll still receive a healthy dose—an additional argument for the already healthy practice of regularly consuming bone broth in your diet.

So Much Healing Potential

A look at how bone broth can have a positive effect on any individual disease or condition could fill an entire book! But this section will give you a good summary of the evidence that supports the use of bone broth for better health. Keep in mind that for any disease or condition you should first consult a health care professional. Discuss with your practitioner the use of bone broth as a part of your prevention or treatment plan.

Inflammatory Disorders

Inflammation is the body's way of responding to dangerous attacks and bringing in resources to fix or rid the body of these hazards. However, diet and environmental contaminants can also cause inflammation in the body. Foods that are filled with preservatives, made from processed vegetable oils, sourced from nonorganic farms, or otherwise exposed to toxins such as chemicals and pesticides can all contribute to chronic inflammation. This is severely detrimental to overall health, not just the affected areas, because it puts the body under constant stress and in perpetual defense mode. Chronic inflammation is often a key symptom of serious illnesses, including diabetes, heart disease, stroke, obesity, arthritis, osteoporosis, cystic fibrosis, fibromyalgia, depression, and anxiety.

Symptoms of chronic inflammation can be controlled with medicine, but not cured. The best way to prevent inflammation is to start with a healthy diet comprised of anti-inflammatory foods. By disrupting the causes of inflammation and removing them from the surrounding environment or regular diet, individuals susceptible to inflammation can prevent it from occurring at all. For those who have lived with chronic inflammation due to poor diet, illness, or environmental contaminants, making healthy lifestyle changes can drastically improve and even repair the damage that has been done to the body.

As a soothing home treatment that has been trusted for generations, bone broth has been proven to reduce, repair, and prevent inflammation and its underlying causes. Paired with healthy eating, regular activity, and awareness of the potential triggers of inflammation, individuals can reduce if not completely rid their lives of these ailments.

Leaky Gut Syndrome

Leaky gut syndrome, while not yet recognized as an official medical condition, is a possible diagnosis proposed in many nutritional circles explaining several long-term and serious illnesses. Advocates of the leaky gut diagnosis suggest that poor diet, infection, alcoholism, certain medications, and parasites can lead to malfunctioning gateways in the gut, perforations in the gut wall, or otherwise compromises in the integrity of the intestinal lining. This breakdown of the intestinal wall can allow dangerous toxins, microbes, and waste to leak through the intestines and enter the bloodstream. The possible symptoms of this disorder are food sensitivities and seasonal allergies; skin conditions such as acne, eczema, and rosacea; gut irritation, including bloating, gas, aches, and even irritable bowel syndrome; hormonal imbalances; and depression and anxiety. More serious reactions may be connected to autoimmune diseases such as lupus, celiac disease, psoriasis, rheumatoid arthritis, and Hashimoto's thyroiditis.

The glutamine in bone broth helps protect the gut lining, which can ameliorate the biggest cause of leaky gut syndrome. As a soothing beverage with anti-inflammatory benefits, bone broth can also reduce the need for anti-inflammatory medications such as ibuprofen that can contribute to these harmful gut perforations.

Celiac Disease

Celiac disease, sometimes known as celiac sprue, is an autoimmune disorder that affects the small intestine. It is caused by a negative reaction to gliadin, a gluten protein that is found in wheat, as well as in some forms of barley and rye. It affects genetically predisposed individuals and occurs somewhere from 1 in 100 to 1 in 170 people, depending on the population. When an affected person ingests gliadin, the immune system and the small-bowel tissue attack one another, which causes an inflammatory response. The symptoms are primarily gastrointestinal, including chronic diarrhea, mouth ulcers, severe abdominal cramping, and bloating. Other more serious side effects include weight loss from the inability to absorb carbohydrates and fat, fatigue, failure to thrive in small children, anemia, and osteoporosis or osteopenia due to a reduced mineral content and weakening in the bones.

A lifelong commitment to healthy foods that do not contain the gluten protein is the only way to avoid the disease's symptoms. While consuming bone broth is not a cure for celiac disease, it is a method of healing the injured intestinal walls of those who suffer from celiac disease.

Small Intestine Bacterial Overgrowth (SIBO)

This is a condition in which the normal homeostasis of the bacteria in the small intestines is disrupted. The gastrointestinal tract is a continuous muscular system that works together to push digesting food through the tract all the way to the colon. While it is normal for the small intestines to contain some forms of bacteria, it is typically in much smaller proportions than in the colon, and a different set of bacteria altogether. In cases of SIBO, the muscular function that assists the movement of food through the digestive tract is interrupted or immobilized, which causes the bacteria in the small intestine to multiply to higher levels than is normal. This pause in muscular movement can also cause the bacteria from the colon to move backward into the small intestine. The abundance of foreign bacteria is toxic to the typically less-bacterial environment of the small intestine. Along with diet changes and the possible use of probiotics, the addition of gentle bone broth to the SIBO sufferer's diet can be miraculously soothing. The anti-inflammatory qualities of the broth can help restore the digestive lining of the intestines, as well as calm the system and return it to its natural balance. In SIBO support communities and in the medical profession, chicken broth is often recommended as a long-term therapy to help heal and keep symptoms at bay.

Irritable Bowel Syndrome (IBS)

Irritable bowel syndrome has similar signs and symptoms as SIBO, but is varied in its causes, diagnosis, and risk factors. Fourteen percent of the U.S. population reports symptoms of IBS, and women are two or three times more likely to be diagnosed with it. The most common complaints associated with IBS are constipation, diarrhea, bloating, excess gas, and severe abdominal pain. While there is no confirmed natural cause of IBS, it is believed that stressful life events, infections, abnormalities in gut flora, and a disruption in communication between the brain and the gastrointestinal tract are most likely to cause it.

The addition of anti-inflammatory foods such as bone broth and other wholesome, organic foods can help relieve symptoms and prevent further gut complications.

Long-Term Benefits of Bone Broth

Need more convincing that bone broth should be a regular part of your daily diet? Along with the disease-fighting benefits of bone broth, there are other ways bone broth can help improve your life and health.

Beauty Boosts

Bone broth's most powerful component affects more than just internal health. Collagen does wonders for overall health, and this can translate to how we age as well. The beauty-boosting possibilities of drinking bone broth daily, as well as incorporating it into other parts of your diet, can have incredible effects on skin, hair, and nails. In a time when both men and women spend thousands of dollars on antiaging treatments—from smoothing wrinkle creams and acne medicines, manicures and pedicures, and shampoo and hair treatments to cosmetics and Botox—a true home remedy that can help ward off skin-deep signs of aging should be priceless. Instead, it is as inexpensive as making dinner.

Higher Energy

The extra boost in energy is just a few daily cups of bone broth away. Not only is the elixir packed with nutrients, minerals, protein, and vitamins that can replenish your system, but also in practice, drinking bone broth can replace some of the drinks that make us lethargic, unmotivated, and less likely to be active. Sugary energy drinks, sodas, and too much caffeine can stimulate momentary rushes of energy, but more often than not, they are followed by intense, regrettable energy crashes and adrenal fatigue. Plus, these kinds of beverages are filled with preservatives, chemicals, and coloring agents that can have severe health consequences, from weight gain and illnesses all the way to cancer. Drinking bone broth is a warm pick-me-up, but its nutrient and protein base sparks energy and jump-starts metabolism. Pair this with supercharged stews and soups made from bone broth, and the medley of vitamins, rich minerals, and nutrition yields a healthy, balanced diet that keeps your system energized.

Better Sleep

Most Americans suffer from sleep deprivation in some form or another. This is a very real problem because the stress on the body associated with lack of sleep can creep into the day, causing fatigue, low energy, and headaches, and can lead to more arduous health problems down the line. The benefits of bone broth to sleep are multifaceted. The first is that with healthy nutrition and bone broth as a part of an active lifestyle, individuals can reduce obesity- and gastrointestinal-related sleep deprivation and have more restful nights. Additionally, the amino acid glycine has been found to facilitate the sleep cycle. Its interaction with brain receptors may be responsible for limiting muscle movement during REM (rapid eye movement) sleep, increasing serotonin levels and lowering core body temperature, all of which promote better sleep.

Cold Fighter

Chicken soup has been the trusted home remedy for cold and flu season for generations. While the reasons behind this have long been anecdotal, researchers may have come up with a scientific explanation. When a cold begins to attack, your body often responds with inflammation as an attempt to defend itself. That includes sending an overload of neutrophils, the most common type of white blood cell, to the respiratory system. A sudden influx of these cells concentrated in this one area can bring on inflammatory symptoms such as a stuffy nose. Recent studies have indicated that chicken soup can inhibit neutrophil migration. The combination of fats and antioxidants in soup made from a whole chicken work together to achieve other health benefits, but the anti-inflammation qualities of chicken soup can deter a number of nutritional deficiencies and sicknesses. Additionally, sipping the warm broth stimulates nasal clearance.

Fitness and Recovery from Injury

Sports and fitness have long been closely linked with high-protein diets, and for good reason. Protein provides energy and helps build muscle, but as a society, we tend to rely on lean cuts of meat and protein powders. While this can have many short-term benefits in the way of muscle building and strength, neglecting the other parts

of the meat that include joint pieces, cartilage, and marrow is a missed opportunity for many reasons. These lesser-chosen parts of the animal provide the vitamins, amino acids, minerals, and fatty acids that lean cuts do not. Not consuming these nutrients can lead to vitamin deficiency and cause harm over the long term. This is where bone broth comes in. The gelatin in bone broth contains many essential amino acids that can help athletes train, compete, and repair the wear and tear on their bodies that can result from intense physical exertion.

Weight Loss

The most healthful elements of bone broth relate to the lifestyle, eating habits, and body healing that it promotes, but it is also a great tool for weight loss (although no individual should look to bone broth alone as a replacement for meals). Broth is the perfect source of nutrition to satisfy and curb hunger until the next meal rather than unhealthy but convenient snacks. The perks of adding bone broth to your diet are that it is low in calories on its own, inexpensive over the long term, simple to make on a daily basis, and has dozens of associated recipes for tonics, soups, stews, and even cocktails to make it an exciting part of your day. The caloric content of 1 cup of beef, chicken, or fish bone broth is between 16 and 30 calories, depending on the ingredients added to the blend.

Tips for the Best Bone Broth

With your Instant Pot and the variety of simple recipes in this book, you have amazing tools on hand to help you make bone broth packed with nutrition and flavor and take advantage of its many health benefits. These expert pointers—from selecting your protein source and bones to storing your broth—can give you even more success with your bone broth batches.

Selecting Your Source

There is an important contributing factor as to why the broth is so healthful and from which all of the health information in the previous sections is based: it is made from organic, grass-fed beef, pasture-raised beef, pork, and poultry, and wild-caught fish. There are dozens of environmental reasons for choosing organic farming over industrialized farming, but for the purposes of nutrition, the saying no longer goes "you are what you eat," but rather, "you are what you eat eats." The process of cooking bone broth concentrates the pesticides and toxins that end up in your meat from conventional farming. This is an important idea to keep in mind when making healthy choices with all food products, whether in terms of what the cattle in your steak ate over the course of its life or the pesticides that are sprayed on the vegetables that end up in your salad.

Grass-Fed

Animals that have spent their lives eating grains like corn instead of grass are at a severe disadvantage. By being given the wrong kind of food for their digestive systems, cattle end up malnourished and lacking important vitamins and minerals. In the cattle industry, allowing cows to graze and eat the healthy grass that their bodies evolved to consume is very expensive. Farmers must own acres upon acres of pasture to make up for how quickly cattle can eat through grassy fields. For the farming industry, the switch to corn feed was an economic decision, not a health one. While this may work for the cattle industry and lower prices of meat for consumers, it creates unhealthy animals, and in turn, unhealthy humans. Corn is a starchy, rich food that fattens cows up quickly, putting meat on American tables significantly faster to meet our high demand. However, cows are not naturally able to digest corn, which builds up a sludge-like material in their stomachs, causes them to bloat, and can put life-threatening strain on their vital organs. In just the same way that juicing nonorganic fruits and vegetables filters pesticides directly into your cup, brewing bone broth with the bones of unhealthy and malnourished animals only concentrates the negative aspects of their diet and brings it directly to yours. Grass-fed cattle have 80 percent less total fat, 30 percent less cholesterol, four times more vitamin E, and ten times more vitamin A than grain-fed cattle do. Grass-fed beef contains omega-3 fatty acids, beta-carotene, and vitamin B6. Not only is grass-fed meat healthier, but it tastes better, too. The meat is leaner and juicier than the greasy and fatty meats of grain-fed beef. By using grass-fed beef bones in your broth, many of the nutrients and positive benefits of a healthy animal will be passed on to your own diet.

Free-Range & Cage-Free vs. Organic & Pasture-Raised

Chicken feet are an amazing source of gelatin, which contributes to making chicken an ideal choice in choosing bones for your broth. Organic, free-range chicken is the best way to reap these health benefits. Here, semantics matter. The terms "free-range" and "cage-free" are popular buzzwords, but do not guarantee healthy chickens on their own. Farms that label themselves as free-range or cage-free do not have to be regulated, meaning that consumers are taking them at their word that the chickens are being well treated, see regular sunlight, and are not confined in close quarters with disease-carrying rodents or in small cages inhaling their own fecal dust for hours of their day.

"Organic," however, is an entirely different story. Farms that are permitted to be official producers of organic poultry are regularly audited by the government and therefore have to follow strict regulations. In order for poultry to meet the USDA's National Organic Standards, poultry must be fed completely organic feed, which means that there are no GMO (genetically modified) crops or animal by-products involved, and no exposure to land that has experienced chemical pesticides or fertilizers in the previous three years. The chickens themselves must be cage-free, have access to the outdoors, and be free of hormones and antibiotics (unless they have been threatened by disease). As a result, using organic chicken bones ensures that your meals and broth will be similarly free of toxins and full of nutrients.

"Pasture-raised" poultry is increasingly popular as well. Many farms that use this term ensure that their chickens spend most, if not all, of their lives with access to the outdoors and are sprout-fed rather than grain-fed. Organic and pasture-raised poultry are your safest bet in finding healthy, nutritious bones for your broth.

Wild-Caught

Using healthy, wild-caught fish in fish-based broths is just as important as using organic meats in meat-based broths. In the open sea and fresh water, fish are free to eat and thrive in their natural ecosystems. Both wild and farm-raised fish have comparable amounts of cholesterol, protein, and magnesium, but wild salmon, for example, has half the fat, less sodium, 32 percent fewer calories, three times less saturated fat, higher amounts of omega 3s, and more zinc, potassium, iron, calcium, and vitamin C than farm-raised fish do. Living conditions are a major concern of farm-raised fish. While the fish being raised in offshore aquaculture may be out in the ocean and not in an industrial plant, they are confined within smaller, netted-off areas that prevent the fish from moving about freely. Overcrowding in these close quarters means that fecal matter and toxins swirl among the confined fish, leading to detrimental infestations and disease. These fish can sometimes escape and spread infections to wild fish in other ecosystems. As a result, this means that fish are given high doses of antibiotics.

Making conscientious choices about where your food products come from is not only healthier for your diet, but also, little by little, it helps propel the food industry into making the right decisions in their food-processing plants and farming to benefit animals and the environment.

Choosing Your Bones

Bones that have high cartilage content, marrow, and gelatin are by far the most important bones to include in your broth because you will see the most nutritional benefits. Beef shank, oxtail, knucklebones, and feet are all concentrated sources of gelatin, which will be released over the course of the long cooking process for making broth. The same goes for pork parts like knucklebones and feet. Including the parts of the animal that are not always used in the modern diet allows us to make use of nose-to-tail-style cooking. While the meat can be cooked in meals, the leftover bones can make nutrient-rich broth that does not let any part of the animal go to waste.

In poultry, the carcass you end up with after roasting a chicken, turkey, or duck is not the only resource for great bone broth; chicken feet and chicken heads are packed with gelatin and good nutrition. While this may come off as unseemly for many people who are not used to seeing chicken feet on their cutting boards, it is both healthful and makes use of the whole animal without wasting parts.

Beef, pork, and poultry bones will have greater potential for releasing gelatin into your broth, but fish bones offer flavor variation and an opportunity not to waste the leftover bones and shells after a meal. The whole carcasses, including the heads, of nonoily fish like snapper and sole, make for delicious fish broth, and so too do shrimp and other shellfish.

If you are cooking bone broth for the first time, start off with an animal whose flavor profile is one you most enjoy cooking and eating. If you are naturally a chicken soup lover, use a whole roasted chicken in your cooking, including the wings and feet. These will bring out the best gelatin content and have flavor potential that you can drink and then use in your cooking. If you are a beef stew connoisseur, in your first batch use beef bones, including marrow and oxtail, which are both nutrient dense and flavorful. A broth with mixed bones, from chicken and turkey bones to pork knuckles and beef marrow, will build complex flavors for a great drinkable broth.

Saving Bones

Preparing bone broth with freshly roasted or raw bones that you get from a butcher, local farmer, or supermarket is always a great choice, but you can also use the bones that you have left over from cooking meals. Any time you roast a chicken, prepare bone-in beef, or roast a whole pig—for the ambitious—wrap up the leftover bones and store them in the freezer. The next time you decide to prepare bone broth, you can use these saved bones and still get the same fantastic nutritional benefits as if you had prepared it the same day. This method prevents waste by presenting the opportunity to use the whole animal, whether it is nose-to-tail or beak-to-tail feather.

Getting the Gel

One of the best markers of nutrient-rich bone broth is that it congeals into a gel-like substance once cooled in the refrigerator. While perhaps unappetizing at first, the gel indicates that the gelatin in the bones, joints, and cartilage pieces that you used during the cooking process has properly made its way into your bone broth. This leads to a super-healthy broth that incorporates all of the health benefits discussed in this book. If the broth does not congeal or thicken when cooled, there are a few things you can do for your next batch that can make all the difference:

1. Add more bones and gristle. You might not have enough of the right kinds of bones in your broth if it is not gelling. Go heavy on the chicken feet, chicken wings, marrowbones, feet or hooves, chicken or fish heads, and even a whole poultry carcass. Using these parts specifically will ensure that the broth you are brewing will be the most potent in nutrients as possible.
2. Use the right kind of bones. If you cheated and used nonorganic beef, poultry, pork, or fish bones, you know where the problem is. It is extremely important that the bones used to make bone broth are from healthy animals. If the animals are malnourished and vitamin deficient, the bone broth will be too.
3. Increase the acid. Specifically in vinegar, acid will help bring out all of the gelatin and minerals in the bones. If you went

light on the vinegar on your first attempt, be sure to add more in your next. While it can smell strong when you first add it, a tablespoon or two more will not make a substantial change in the flavor or aroma of the overall broth. If you have a strong distaste of vinegar or are wary of using too much vinegar that might exacerbate any sensitivities you may have, then replace the vinegar with citrus such as lemon juice.

How Your Instant Pot Helps

With so much goodness packed into bone broth, there's no reason why a busy schedule should hold you back from enjoying it. While making your own bone broth using an Instant Pot isn't quite "instant," it's definitely more achievable than making bone broth the old-fashioned stovetop way that can take from 4 to 24 hours, with a lot of stirring and monitoring during that time. You'll also get more consistent results with the Instant Pot. Your broth won't turn bitter (especially when adding vegetables) or lose liquid during the cooking process.

The Method Behind the Magic

Each recipe in this book utilizes the Instant Pot as its main method of cooking. The Instant Pot is a jack-of-all-trades when it comes to kitchen appliances. It's an automatic multi-cooker that can be used in many ways: as an electric pressure cooker, a steamer, a slow cooker, a sauté/browning pan, a yogurt maker, a rice steamer, and more. In most instances, the Instant Pot accomplishes cooking tasks two to six times quicker and with considerably less fuss and mess than traditional stovetop or oven cooking methods. The magic is in the pressure function, which cooks foods at a lower temperature but at a higher pressure. This technique allows for previously unachievable cooking times. The best part is that the Instant Pot is a kitchen shortcut that doesn't affect quality, nutritional value, or, best of all, taste.

Another plus: you don't have to monitor the Instant Pot. Just press the right button, make sure the valve is sealed, and enjoy time for yourself or with your family while the Instant Pot cooks up something delicious. Program function keys are designed to provide consistent results. However, you can also use the manual setting, which is what we use for many of the recipes in this book.

Simply press Manual, adjust the time using the – and + buttons, and that's it. Nothing could be simpler than pressing a button and walking away until you hear the Instant Pot beep, announcing that your bone broth is ready! The Keep Warm/Cancel button will keep the food warm after the cooking is completed. You'll find using the Instant Pot to be very simple, but it's still a good idea to read the instruction manual before using your cooker for the recipes in this book.

The one downside of using an Instant Pot is that, even with the largest 8-quart pot (the recipes in this book use the more popular 6-quart size), you won't be making tons of broth with each session. Also, the bones may need to be cut into smaller pieces to fit in the cooker. The time you save, however, will more than make up for this minor shortcoming.

Flavor under Pressure

When used as a pressure cooker, the Instant Pot not only cooks and tenderizes the food, but also retains all the vitamins and minerals in whatever you're cooking. As a fully sealed environment for your cooking, all the flavor stays right where it belongs as well.

The Instant Pot will not start pressure cooking until the lid is closed properly. (You can use the Sauté setting and keep food warm without the lid.) The lid has a steam valve, which allows the pressure cooker to either build or release pressure. When pressure cooking, make sure the valve is in the sealing position. Also, when you start the pressure cooker, know that it takes anywhere from 3 to 10 minutes for the pressure to build up. Take that into consideration when estimating cooking times.

When the time is up on your Instant Pot meal, the Instant Pot will automatically change to the Keep Warm function and will gradually begin to lose pressure. It can take a while for the pressure to fully release naturally—up to 30 minutes. Most of the recipes in this book call for up to 10 minutes of waiting for the pressure to release naturally before turning the steam valve to "venting." The best way to do this is to use a kitchen towel or an oven mitt.

More Pressure Pointers

- Put the inner pot in the Instant Pot before using. You can damage the Instant Pot by pouring liquids into the main pot.
- Keep the contents at least 1 inch below the maximum fill line. If cooking foods that will expand (rice, beans, etc.), don't even go two-thirds full.
- Make sure the venting knob is in the sealing position. The floating valve will pop up. If you don't see that, fix it.
- Keep in mind that higher altitudes may require longer cooking times. A good guideline is to extend the pressure time 5 percent for every 1,000 feet above sea level.
- While it's fine to remove the sealing ring from the lid to wash it (in fact, you should to that after every time you use it), don't forget to put it back in before using the Instant Pot.

Smart Storage

Perhaps the easiest way to incorporate bone broth into your daily diet is to make batches of it ahead of time, as the Basic Bone Broths in this cookbook (beginning on page 37) help you do. These broths come together so quickly in the Instant Pot with very little hands-on time needed. Then just store them in your refrigerator or freezer until you want to enjoy as a stand-alone drink or use in a dinner recipe. A few hints will help you get the best results.

Go for Glass

Glass containers like mason jars and Pyrex bowls are ideal for storing broth. Large mason jars are great sizes for portioning broth for soups, and small glass jelly or sauce jars are the perfect size for individual cups of drinking broth. These can be reused over and over again and washed in the dishwasher, making cleanup and continuous broth storage incredibly easy. Metal lids on mason jars have a tendency to rust over time, so it is a good idea to purchase plastic replacement lids that screw right onto mason jars. For glass jars that close with clamps, replacement rubber gaskets for worn-out ones can be found at any hardware store or online.

Freeze with Ease

When freezing bone broth in glass jars, the most important thing to remember is to leave at least 2 inches between the broth and the lid. Liquid expands when frozen, which can cause full jars to shatter. In just the same way that hot beverage glasses right from the dishwasher can break when filled with cold liquid or ice, breakage can happen when transferring the jar from hot to cold locations. Be sure to allow the broth to cool to room temperature before storing it in the freezer, or refrigerate for a day and remove the fat from the top prior to freezing. This step will minimize shatter risk and make the thawing process significantly easier.

Use Ice Cube Trays

A great time-saver and recipe trick, pouring reduced bone broth into ice cube trays and freezing them is a resourceful method to season or add moisture to any meal. Whether you are roasting vegetables or making brown rice, bone broth cubes can add just the right amount of flavor. Take a couple of cubes of reduced bone broth and heat them in a saucepan prior to incorporating them into your cooking. Cover the trays with plastic wrap or parchment paper so that they remain separate from other ice trays in your freezer.

You can refrigerate bone broth in airtight containers for up to 5 days or freeze for up to 6 months. When you want to use, simply let it come to room temperature or heat it a little until it is no longer gelled. It's that simple.

PART 2

Recipes for Flavor & Health

Basic Bone Broths

The nutrient-packed recipes featured in this section represent what are called neutral broths. These bone broths are super versatile! They have a very mild flavor that you can enjoy straight up. (If you're looking for bolder flavor, check out the broths in the next section, Drinks & Tonics.) Neutral broths can also be used to strengthen the nutritional profile of any recipe that calls for basic broth or even water. Keep some on hand to use in the recipes throughout this book or in your own favorite recipes.

Basic Beef Bone Broth

This variation may be the most commonly used of all bone broths. Its nutrient profile is the densest; grass-fed beef contains conjugated linoleic acid (CLA), alpha-linolenic acid (ALA), and omega-3s, all beneficial fatty acids with strong anti-inflammatory properties. The classic flavor is easy to work into any meaty recipe once the broth is made.

Makes approximately 3 quarts

Ingredients
1 tablespoon olive oil (optional)

3 pounds grass-fed beef marrow bones, raw or cooked leftovers

3 quarts water

2 tablespoons apple cider vinegar

1 tablespoon salt

TIP
Want to make a different quantity? For any of the basic recipes in this section, simply use the ratio of 1 pound bones to 1 quart water, with 1 teaspoon salt and ½ tablespoon apple cider vinegar per pound of bones.

Instructions
1. If the bones are raw, brown them first, if desired, to increase flavor. To do that, add the olive oil to the Instant Pot and press Sauté. When hot, add the bones in batches and cook for 5 minutes, or until browned on all sides.
2. Place the bones in a 6-quart Instant Pot along with the water, vinegar, and salt. Check that the liquid level is at least 1 inch below the maximum fill line. Lock the lid and make sure the valve is sealed.
3. Press Soup/Broth and adjust the time to 120 minutes.
4. When the cook time is complete, turn off the Instant Pot and let the pressure release naturally for 5 to 10 minutes before turning the valve to venting. Then, remove the lid.
5. Strain the broth through a fine-mesh strainer or cheesecloth set over a bowl. Discard the solids. Transfer the broth to a few different containers so it will cool faster.
6. When the broth is cool enough to handle, refrigerate uncovered for several hours, or until the fat rises to the top. Scrape off the fat and discard it.
7. Refrigerate in airtight containers for up to 5 days or freeze for up to 6 months.

Basic Chicken Bone Broth

Chicken broth is universally comforting and has excellent immune-boosting properties. The flavor is distinct yet can easily be drawn into the background of other recipes to add an umami quality.

Makes approximately 3 quarts

Ingredients

1 large chicken carcass or 3 pounds chicken necks, backs, and/or feet, broken up to release marrow

3 quarts water

2 tablespoons apple cider vinegar

1 tablespoon salt

Instructions

1. Place the chicken bones in a 6-quart Instant Pot along with the water, vinegar, and salt. Check that the liquid level is at least 1 inch below the maximum fill line. Lock the lid and make sure the valve is sealed.
2. Press Soup/Broth and adjust the time to 120 minutes.
3. When the cook time is complete, turn off the Instant Pot and let the pressure release naturally for 5 to 10 minutes before turning the valve to venting. Then, remove the lid.
4. Strain the broth through a fine-mesh strainer or cheesecloth set over a bowl. Discard the solids. Transfer the broth to a few different containers so it will cool faster.
5. When the broth is cool enough to handle, refrigerate uncovered for several hours, or until the fat rises to the top. Scrape off the fat and discard it.
6. Refrigerate in airtight containers for up to 5 days or freeze for up to 6 months.

Basic Lamb Bone Broth

Lamb is packed with B vitamins, zinc, and even more CLA than beef. Although the aroma can be strong, its gentle flavor makes it a great base for all sorts of seasoning combinations.

Makes approximately 3 quarts

Ingredients

1 tablespoon olive oil (optional)
3 pounds lamb marrowbones,
   raw or cooked leftovers
3 quarts water
2 tablespoons apple cider vinegar
1 tablespoon salt

Instructions

1. If the bones are raw, brown them first, if desired, to increase flavor. To do that, add the olive oil to the Instant Pot and press Sauté. When hot, add the bones in batches and cook for 5 minutes, or until browned on all sides.
2. Place the bones in a 6-quart Instant Pot along with the water, vinegar, and salt. Check that the liquid level is at least 1 inch below the maximum fill line. Lock the lid and make sure the valve is sealed.
3. Press Soup/Broth and adjust the time to 120 minutes.
4. When the cook time is complete, turn off the Instant Pot and let the pressure release naturally for 5 to 10 minutes before turning the valve to venting. Then, remove the lid.
5. Strain the broth through a fine-mesh strainer or cheesecloth set over a bowl. Discard the solids. Transfer the broth to a few different containers so it will cool faster.
6. When the broth is cool enough to handle, refrigerate uncovered for several hours, or until the fat rises to the top. Scrape off the fat and discard it.
7. Refrigerate in airtight containers for up to 5 days or freeze for up to 6 months.

Basic Fish Bone Broth

Fish has such a different profile from poultry or red meat that it's an excellent way to switch up flavors and cover your nutritional bases. Because the bones and fats in fish are delicate, you will cook this broth for a much shorter time compared to the other basic broths to extract the benefits and keep the flavor mild.

Makes approximately 3 quarts

Ingredients
3 pounds fish heads and carcasses,
    raw or cooked leftovers
3 quarts water
2 tablespoons apple cider vinegar
½ tablespoon salt

Instructions
1. If the fish heads are raw, wash them first until all the blood is removed.
2. Place the heads and bones in a 6-quart Instant Pot along with the water, vinegar, and salt. Check that the liquid level is at least 1 inch below the maximum fill line. Lock the lid and make sure the valve is sealed.
3. Press Soup/Broth and adjust the time to 15 minutes.
4. When the cook time is complete, turn off the Instant Pot and let the pressure release naturally for 5 to 10 minutes before turning the valve to venting. Then, remove the lid.
5. Strain the broth through a fine-mesh strainer or cheesecloth set over a bowl. Discard the solids. Transfer the broth to a few different containers so it will cool faster.
6. When the broth is cool enough to handle, refrigerate uncovered for several hours, or until the fat rises to the top. Scrape off the fat and discard it.
7. Refrigerate in airtight containers for up to 5 days or freeze for up to 6 months.

Mixed Poultry Bone Broth

Chicken is the perfect poultry go-to for broth, but there is plenty to gain by changing out your bird bones. Duck offers zinc and selenium, and turkey is chock-full of B vitamins. Because chicken, duck, and turkey have distinctly different tastes, combining the three will yield a flavorful broth that's still versatile.

Makes approximately 3 quarts

Ingredients

3 pounds chicken, duck, and/or turkey
   bones, raw or cooked leftovers
3 quarts water
2 tablespoons apple cider vinegar
1 tablespoon salt

Instructions

1. Place the bones in a 6-quart Instant Pot along with the water, vinegar, and salt. Check that the liquid level is at least 1 inch below the maximum fill line. Lock the lid and make sure the valve is sealed.
2. Press Soup/Broth and adjust the time to 120 minutes.
3. When the cook time is complete, turn off the Instant Pot and let the pressure release naturally for 5 to 10 minutes before turning the valve to venting. Then, remove the lid.
4. Strain the broth through a fine-mesh strainer or cheesecloth set over a bowl. Discard the solids. Transfer the broth to a few different containers so it will cool faster.
5. When the broth is cool enough to handle, refrigerate uncovered for several hours, or until the fat rises to the top. Scrape off the fat and discard it.
6. Refrigerate in airtight containers for up to 5 days or freeze for up to 6 months.

Herb & Vegetable Beef Bone Broth

This recipe is the Basic Beef Bone Broth (page 39) dressed up a bit. Try creating even more flavorful beef varieties simply by switching up the herbs and vegetables you add to the pot. You'll discover so many delicious broths you can drink as is or use in recipes.

Makes approximately 3 quarts

Ingredients

1 tablespoon olive oil (optional)

3 pounds grass-fed beef marrowbones, raw or cooked leftovers

3 quarts water

1 pound portobello mushrooms, chopped

4 cloves garlic, chopped

4 celery ribs

2 yellow onions, peeled and chopped

2 carrots, peeled and chopped

2 tablespoons apple cider vinegar

1 tablespoon dried sage

1 tablespoon dried thyme

1 tablespoon dried oregano

1 tablespoon salt

Instructions

1. If the bones are raw, brown first them, if desired, to increase flavor. To do that, add the oil to the Instant Pot and press Sauté. When hot, add the bones in batches and cook for 5 minutes, or until browned on all sides.
2. Place the bones in a 6-quart Instant Pot along with the rest of the ingredients. Check that the water is at least 1 inch below the maximum fill line. Lock the lid and make sure the valve is sealed.
3. Press Soup/Broth and adjust the time to 120 minutes.
4. When the cook time is complete, turn off the Instant Pot and let the pressure release naturally for 5 to 10 minutes before turning the valve to venting. Then, remove the lid.
5. Strain the broth through a fine-mesh strainer or cheesecloth set over a bowl. Discard the solids. Transfer the broth to a few different containers so it will cool faster.
6. When the broth is cool enough to handle, refrigerate uncovered for several hours, or until the fat rises to the top. Scrape off the fat and discard it.
7. Refrigerate in airtight containers for up to 5 days or freeze for up to 6 months.

Thanksgiving Turkey Bone Broth

With this recipe you can savor the taste and nutrition of turkey, herbs, and root vegetables beyond Thanksgiving dinner—and without the tempting extra calories from rich sides. Simply drink in a feast of nutrients.

Makes approximately 3 quarts

Ingredients

3 pounds leftover turkey bones, broken
    into smaller pieces when necessary
3 quarts water
4 cloves garlic, chopped
4 celery ribs, chopped
3 carrots, peeled and chopped
2 red onions, chopped
3 cups chopped fresh basil
1 cup crushed caraway seeds
½ cup chopped sage
2 tablespoons apple cider vinegar
1 tablespoon salt

Instructions

1. Place the ingredients in a 6-quart Instant Pot. Check that the liquid level is at least 1 inch below the maximum fill line. Lock the lid and make sure the valve is sealed.
2. Press Soup/Broth and adjust the time to 120 minutes.
3. When the cook time is complete, turn off the Instant Pot and let the pressure release naturally for 5 to 10 minutes before turning the valve to venting. Then, remove the lid.
4. Strain the broth through a fine-mesh strainer or cheesecloth set over a bowl. Discard the solids. Transfer the broth to a few different containers so it will cool faster.
5. When the broth is cool enough to handle, refrigerate uncovered for several hours, or until the fat rises to the top. Scrape off the fat and discard it.
6. Refrigerate in airtight containers for up to 5 days or freeze for up to 6 months.

Vegetable & Chicken Bone Broth

The more you use your Instant Pot to make bone broths, the longer your list of variations will grow. Experimentation will almost always yield something interesting to use in other recipes or to drink on its own. Replace the veggies you don't care for in this recipe with others you like, and have fun!

Makes approximately 3 quarts

Ingredients

1 large chicken carcass or 3 pounds chicken necks, backs, and/or feet, broken up to release marrow

3 quarts water

3 tablespoons freshly squeezed lemon juice

3 cloves garlic, chopped

3 celery ribs, chopped

2 large carrots, peeled and chopped

1 zucchini, sliced

1½ cups fresh or frozen green peas

1½ cups fresh or frozen corn kernels

2 tablespoons apple cider vinegar

1 bay leaf

1 tablespoon salt

Instructions

1. Place the ingredients in a 6-quart Instant Pot. Check that the liquid level is at least 1 inch below the maximum fill line. Lock the lid and make sure the valve is sealed.

2. Press Soup/Broth and adjust the time to 120 minutes.

3. When the cook time is complete, turn off the Instant Pot and let the pressure release naturally for 5 to 10 minutes before turning the valve to venting. Then, remove the lid.

4. Strain the broth through a fine-mesh strainer or cheesecloth set over a bowl. Discard the solids. Transfer the broth to a few different containers so it will cool faster.

5. When the broth is cool enough to handle, refrigerate uncovered for several hours, or until the fat rises to the top. Scrape off the fat and discard it.

6. Refrigerate in airtight containers for up to 5 days or freeze for up to 6 months.

Drinks & Tonics

Now that you have the basics in your repertoire, you're ready to take your bone broth experiences up a notch with more complex drinkable broths, tonics you start from premade broths, and even cocktails you can make with broth. These recipes give you new, delicious options for getting your daily intake of bone broth. Keep in mind: when using premade bone broth as part of a recipe, you may need to let it come to room temperature or heat it a little until it is no longer gelled.

Curried Vegetable Chicken Bone Broth

Curry powder—the Indian spice blend that features coriander, cumin, and turmeric, among other spices—captures your attention with its flavor. It is also worth your attention due to a component in turmeric called curcumin, which is believed to have anti-inflammatory, antioxidant, and possibly even anticancer properties.

Makes 8–10 servings

Ingredients

1 chicken carcass or 3 pounds chicken necks, backs, and/or feet, broken up to release marrow

3 quarts water

4 celery ribs, leaves intact

4 cloves garlic

3 carrots, peeled and chopped

2 yellow onions, chopped

2 tablespoons apple cider vinegar

2 tablespoons dried thyme

2 tablespoons curry powder

1 tablespoon salt

1 teaspoon ground nutmeg

Instructions

1. Place the ingredients in a 6-quart Instant Pot. Check that the water is at least 1 inch below the maximum fill line. Lock the lid and make sure the valve is sealed.
2. Press Soup/Broth and adjust the time to 120 minutes.
3. When the cook time is complete, turn off the Instant Pot and let the pressure release naturally for 5 to 10 minutes before turning the valve to venting. Then, remove the lid.
4. Strain the broth through a fine-mesh strainer or cheesecloth set over a bowl. Discard the solids.
5. Drink hot or refrigerate in airtight containers for up to 5 days or freeze for up to 6 months.

Thai Chicken Bone Broth

Wake up your taste buds with this broth that you can drink as is or add to your next Thai-based soup or stew. Lemongrass brings a bright flavor to the broth, as well as antioxidant and anti-inflammatory properties. Yellow miso lends amazing umami that deepens the taste but is mild enough to never steal the show.

Makes 8–10 servings

Ingredients
1 chicken carcass or 3 pounds chicken
   necks, backs, and/or feet,
   broken up to release marrow
3 quarts water
4 cloves garlic, chopped
4 cups chopped lemongrass
2–3 green onions, chopped
1-inch piece ginger, sliced into rounds
½ cup yellow miso paste
2 tablespoons apple cider vinegar
2–3 cilantro sprigs
1 tablespoon salt

Instructions
1. Place the ingredients in a 6-quart Instant Pot. Check that the water is at least 1 inch below the maximum fill line. Lock the lid and make sure the valve is sealed.
2. Press Soup/Broth and adjust the time to 120 minutes.
3. When the cook time is complete, turn off the Instant Pot and let the pressure release naturally for 5 to 10 minutes before turning the valve to venting. Then, remove the lid.
4. Strain the broth through a fine-mesh strainer or cheesecloth set over a bowl. Discard the solids.
5. Drink hot or refrigerate in airtight containers for up to 5 days or freeze for up to 6 months.

Lemon-Tarragon Chicken Bone Broth

A classic ingredient in French cuisine, tarragon is a slightly bittersweet herb with an aroma similar to anise. It pairs perfectly with lemon and garlic as a poultry seasoning. Tarragon's benefits beyond flavor include the potential to calm digestive troubles and promote better sleep.

Makes 8–10 servings

Ingredients

1 chicken carcass or 3 pounds chicken
    necks, backs, and/or feet,
    broken up to release marrow
3 quarts water
4 cloves garlic
1 onion, chopped
2 tablespoons apple cider vinegar
2 tablespoons dried tarragon
1 tablespoon salt
¼ cup freshly squeezed lemon juice

Instructions

1. Place all the ingredients except for the lemon juice in a 6-quart Instant Pot. Check that the water is at least 1 inch below the maximum fill line. Lock the lid and make sure the valve is sealed.
2. Press Soup/Broth and adjust the time to 120 minutes.
3. When the cook time is complete, turn off the Instant Pot and let the pressure release naturally for 5 to 10 minutes before turning the valve to venting. Then, remove the lid and let cool for 20 minutes. Add the lemon juice and stir.
4. Strain the broth through a fine-mesh strainer or cheesecloth set over a bowl. Discard the solids.
5. Drink immediately or refrigerate in airtight containers for up to 5 days or freeze for up to 6 months.

Tomato-Based Beef Bone Broth

Take your tomato juice to a whole new level with this beef bone broth recipe that includes 8 cups of tomato puree! Along with all the nutritional gifts of the bone broth, you'll get vitamin C and lycopene from the tomatoes. You can make the puree at home or purchase a brand without added sugar. For an extra kick of flavor, add a little Tabasco sauce.

Makes 8–10 servings

Ingredients

2 pounds beef marrowbones, raw
   or cooked leftovers
8 cups water
8 cups tomato puree
4 cloves garlic, chopped
2 onions, chopped
3 cups chopped fresh basil
2 tablespoons apple cider vinegar
2 bay leaves
Salt and pepper, to taste

Instructions

1. Place the ingredients in a 6-quart Instant Pot. Check that the liquid is at least 1 inch below the maximum fill line. Lock the lid and make sure the valve is sealed.
2. Press Soup/Broth and adjust the time to 120 minutes.
3. When the cook time is complete, turn off the Instant Pot and let the pressure release naturally for 5 to 10 minutes before turning the valve to venting. Then, remove the lid.
4. Strain the broth through a fine-mesh strainer or cheesecloth set over a bowl. Discard the solids.
5. Drink hot or refrigerate in airtight containers for up to 5 days or freeze for up to 6 months.

Digestive Double-Team Bone Broth

Bone broth is amazingly beneficial for digestion because of how well the gelatin can soothe and heal your intestines. Adding beets boosts the digestive benefits because the root vegetables contain betaine, which stimulates bile production. Even their bitter greens contribute; bitter foods stimulate the production of digestive juices in the stomach.

Makes 8–10 servings

Ingredients

1 tablespoon olive oil (optional)
3 pounds salmon, chicken, or beef bones, raw or cooked leftovers
3 quarts water
3 medium beets, cut into ½-inch cubes
Greens from 3 beets, sliced or whole
2 medium zucchini, sliced into ¾-inch rounds
2 tablespoons apple cider vinegar
1 tablespoon salt

TIP

If you would rather make a different quantity, use the ratio of 1 pound bones to 1 quart water, with ½ zucchini, 1 small beet root with greens, 1 teaspoon salt, and ½ tablespoon vinegar per pound of bones.

Instructions

1. If the bones are raw, brown them first, if desired, to increase flavor. To do that, add the oil to the Instant Pot and press Sauté. When hot, add the bones in batches and cook for 5 minutes, or until browned on all sides.
2. Place the ingredients in a 6-quart Instant Pot. Check that the water is at least 1 inch below the maximum fill line. Lock the lid and make sure the valve is sealed.
3. Press Soup/Broth and adjust the time to 120 minutes.
4. When the cook time is complete, turn off the Instant Pot and let the pressure release naturally for 5 to 10 minutes before turning the valve to venting. Then, remove the lid.
5. Strain the broth through a fine-mesh strainer or cheesecloth set over a bowl. Discard the solids. Transfer the broth to a few different containers so it will cool faster.
6. When the broth is cool enough to handle, refrigerate uncovered for several hours, or until the fat rises to the top. Scrape off the fat and discard it.
7. Refrigerate in airtight containers for up to 5 days or freeze for up to 6 months.

Beauty Wonder Bone Broth

While all bone broths contain collagen and help contribute to your body's own collagen production, this broth is the fast track there. Chicken and pig feet are dense with collagen, and lycopene-rich red foods such as tomatoes and hot peppers help your body create even more. The flavor of these bones is surprisingly mild, so the tomatoes actually play a larger role in the taste.

Makes 8–10 servings

Ingredients

1 tablespoon olive oil (optional)
1½ pounds chicken feet
2 pig feet
3 quarts water
8 ounces tomatoes, halved

1 hot red pepper, with or without seeds, halved (optional)
1 tablespoon apple cider vinegar
½ tablespoon salt

Instructions

1. If the chicken and pig feet are raw, brown them first, if desired, to increase flavor. To do that, add the oil to the Instant Pot and press Sauté. When hot, add the feet in batches and cook for 5 minutes, or until browned on all sides.
2. Place all the ingredients in a 6-quart Instant Pot. Check that the water is at least 1 inch below the maximum fill line. Lock the lid and make sure the valve is sealed.
3. Press Soup/Broth and adjust the time to 120 minutes.
4. When the cook time is complete, turn off the Instant Pot and let the pressure release naturally for 5 to 10 minutes before turning the valve to venting. Then, remove the lid.
5. Strain the broth through a fine-mesh strainer or cheesecloth set over a bowl. Discard the solids. Transfer the broth to a few different containers so it will cool faster.
6. When the broth is cool enough to handle, refrigerate uncovered for several hours, or until the fat rises to the top. Scrape off the fat and discard it.
7. Refrigerate in airtight containers for up to 5 days or freeze for up to 6 months.

Immune System Powerhouse Bone Broth

Any basic chicken bone broth offers immune system benefits, but you can strengthen that power with a few targeted ingredients. This broth is designed to help knock colds and flu out of your system, rather than them knocking you on your back for days. With immune-boosting mushrooms, garlic, and oregano, the broth may be pungent, but it tastes much better than cough syrup.

Makes 8–10 servings

Ingredients

1 tablespoon olive oil (optional)

3 pounds chicken backs, necks, or other bones, raw or cooked leftovers

3 quarts water

5 ounces dried shiitake mushrooms, reconstituted in hot water

1 garlic bulb, sliced in half through the center

1½ tablespoons apple cider vinegar

3 sprigs fresh oregano

½ tablespoon salt

Instructions

1. If the bones are raw, brown them first, if desired, to increase flavor. To do that, add the oil to the Instant Pot and press Sauté. When hot, add the bones in batches and cook for 5 minutes, or until browned on all sides. If using chicken backs, drain the oil after browning.
2. Place the ingredients in a 6-quart Instant Pot. Check that the water is at least 1 inch below the maximum fill line. Lock the lid and make sure the valve is sealed.
3. Press Soup/Broth and adjust the time to 120 minutes.
4. When the cook time is complete, turn off the Instant Pot and let the pressure release naturally for 5 to 10 minutes before turning the valve to venting. Then, remove the lid.
5. Strain the broth through a fine-mesh strainer or cheesecloth set over a bowl. Discard the solids. Transfer the broth to a few different containers so it will cool faster.
6. When the broth is cool enough to handle, refrigerate uncovered for several hours or until the fat rises to the top. Scrape off the fat and discard it.
7. Refrigerate in airtight containers for up to 5 days or freeze for up to 6 months.

Inflammation-Taming Bone Broth

All bone broth made from grass-fed meat and wild fish will help reduce inflammation. But, if inflammation is currently nagging your health and getting in the way of enjoying your life, you may want to amp up your defenses and tackle it as fiercely as possible. Packed with powerfully calming ginger, turmeric, and sweet potatoes, this recipe battles back and soothes your system.

Makes 8–10 servings

Ingredients

1 tablespoon olive oil (optional)

3 pounds beef or lamb marrowbones, raw or cooked leftovers

3 quarts water

2 tablespoons apple cider vinegar

1 tablespoon salt

3 inches ginger, sliced into ¼-inch rounds

1 small sweet potato, cut into quarters

4 fresh turmeric roots, sliced lengthwise

Instructions

1. If the bones are raw, brown them first, if desired, to increase flavor. To do that, add the oil to the Instant Pot, and press Sauté. When hot, add the bones in batches and cook for 5 minutes or until browned on all sides.
2. Place the ingredients in a 6-quart Instant Pot. Check that the water is at least 1 inch below the maximum fill line. Lock the lid and make sure the valve is sealed.
3. Press Soup/Broth and adjust the time to 120 minutes.
4. When the cook time is complete, turn off the Instant Pot and let the pressure release naturally for 5 to 10 minutes before turning the valve to venting. Then, remove the lid.
5. Strain the broth through a fine-mesh strainer or cheesecloth set over a bowl. Discard the solids. Transfer the broth to a few different containers so it will cool faster.
6. When the broth is cool enough to handle, refrigerate uncovered for several hours, or until the fat rises to the top. Scrape off the fat and discard it.
7. Refrigerate in airtight containers for up to 5 days or freeze for up to 6 months.

TIP: If you would rather make a different quantity, use the ratio of 1 pound bones to 1 quart water, with 1-inch piece ginger, 1 turmeric root, ½ sweet potato, 1 teaspoon salt, and ½ tablespoon vinegar per pound of bones.

Mood-Boosting Bone Broth

If you have tried bone broth before, you already know that it can provide a surprisingly hefty amount of bioavailable energy. With the additions of lemongrass for lift and asparagus for a hit of folate and tryptophan, the feel-good nature of broth becomes even more amazing in this bone broth recipe.

Makes 8–10 servings

Ingredients
1 tablespoon olive oil (optional)
3 pounds chicken, salmon, or beef bones,
    raw or cooked leftovers
3 quarts water
3 inches lemongrass, broken or cut in half
½ bunch asparagus, cut into thirds
1 tablespoon apple cider vinegar
½ tablespoon salt

Instructions
1. If the bones are raw, brown them first, if desired, to increase flavor. To do that, add the oil to the Instant Pot and press Sauté. When hot, add the bones in batches and cook for 5 minutes, or until browned on all sides.
2. Place the ingredients in a 6-quart Instant Pot. Check that the water is at least 1 inch below the maximum fill line. Lock the lid and make sure the valve is sealed.
3. Press Soup/Broth and adjust the time to 120 minutes.
4. When the cook time is complete, turn off the Instant Pot and let the pressure release naturally for 5 to 10 minutes before turning the valve to venting. Then, remove the lid.
5. Strain the broth through a fine-mesh strainer or cheesecloth set over a bowl. Discard the solids. Transfer the broth to a few different containers so it will cool faster.
6. When the broth is cool enough to handle, refrigerate uncovered for several hours, or until the fat rises to the top. Scrape off the fat and discard it.
7. Refrigerate in airtight containers for up to 5 days or freeze for up to 6 months.

Ginger Head-to-Toe Health Tonic

Ginger is one of the healthiest of spices, with benefits that include increased blood flow, better digestion, anti-inflammatory and pain-relieving properties, blood sugar balance, and improved memory. Both ginger and cayenne pepper have immune-boosting properties. Pair those spices with bone broth, and you have so much health power in one mug!

Makes 2 servings

Ingredients
2 cups Basic Chicken Bone Broth (page 41)
2 tablespoons grated ginger
Juice of 1 lemon
⅛ teaspoon cayenne pepper
Salt, to taste

Instructions
1. Heat all the ingredients in a small saucepan until very warm.
2. Serve hot, at room temperature, or cold.

Energy-on-Ice Broth-ee

Sure, you can simply add hot bone broth to your morning coffee. But why not try this creamy smoothie for a deliciously different way to take in the bone broth energy that will sustain you throughout the day? For an extra jolt of caffeine, replace the coffee with a couple shots of espresso.

Makes 2 servings

Ingredients

½ cup brewed coffee
½ cup milk
½ cup Basic Chicken Bone Broth (page 41),
    frozen into cubes (see Tip, page 69)
1 frozen banana
1 tablespoon cocoa powder (optional)

Instructions

1. Place all the ingredients in a blender and blend until smooth.

Green Monster Smoothie

With spinach and avocado alone, there's so much nutrition in this green package! You can experiment with how much bone broth to add to this recipe, but make sure you use one of the more neutral broths such as the Basic Beef Bone Broth (page 39) or the Basic Chicken Bone Broth (page 41).

Makes 2 servings

Ingredients
2 cups spinach
1 Granny Smith apple
½ banana
½ avocado
½ cup (or less) water
¼ cup (or more) Basic Beef Bone Broth (page 39),
    frozen into cubes*
¼ cup almond butter
1 tablespoon ground cinnamon
2 teaspoons honey
1 teaspoon chia seeds
Salt, to taste

TIP
Buy an ice cube tray especially for bone broth cubes, which are great to mix into smoothies or to cool off soup.

Instructions
1. Place all the ingredients in a blender and blend until smooth.
2. Adjust the honey or other ingredients as needed.

Stress-Battling Berry Smoothie

All berries are beneficial for your health, but blueberries, blackberries, and raspberries have some of the highest antioxidant activity among fruits. Partner them with bone broth, and you're giving your body superpower to fight oxidative stress. If bone broth added to a fruit smoothie is new to your taste buds, you can start with 1 ounce of broth the first time you make this blend and build up to adding more. If you want to go beyond 4 ounces of bone broth, simply add less water.

Makes 1 serving

Ingredients
4 ounces Basic Chicken Bone Broth (page 41),
    frozen into cubes (see Tip, page 69)
1 frozen banana
1 cup mixed berries
½ cup water
¼ cup flaxseeds, hemp seeds, and/or chia seeds
Fresh mint, for garnish (optional)

Instructions
1. Place all the ingredients in a blender and blend until smooth. Garnish with mint, if using.

Bone Broth–Turmeric Latte

Looking to power up your mind and body without caffeine? This rich-tasting, energy-boosting "latte" skips the caffeine but provides the healthy fats needed for you to make it through the day at your best. Curcumin in the turmeric adds anti-inflammatory properties.

Makes 1 serving

Ingredients
1 cup Basic Chicken Bone Broth (page 41)
1 tablespoon coconut oil
1 tablespoon grated ginger
1 tablespoon unsalted butter or ghee
½ teaspoon lemon juice
¼ teaspoon turmeric
¼ teaspoon ground cinnamon

Instructions
1. Place the broth in a saucepan and bring to a simmer.
2. Pour it into a blender with the rest of the ingredients and blend until frothy.

Ultimate Anti-Inflammatory Tonic

If the Inflammation-Taming Bone Broth (page 63) isn't doing the trick for you, use the broth in this tonic during a flare-up. During a time of discomfort, a soothing anti-inflammatory drink can bring almost immediate relief. The gelatin powder will soothe the lining of your digestive tract while making your nails, hair, and skin look marvelous!

Makes 1 serving

Ingredients

1 cup Inflammation-Taming Bone Broth (page 63),
    Basic Beef Bone Broth (page 39),
    or Basic Lamb Bone Broth (page 42)
2 tablespoons freshly grated turmeric root
1 tablespoon freshly grated ginger
1 tablespoon gelatin powder

Instructions

1. Heat all the ingredients in a saucepan until the tonic is very warm and the gelatin has dissolved.

Cough-Quieting Tonic

Although thyme's leaves are tiny, the herb packs powerful compounds that relax muscles involved in coughing and also calm inflammation, making it an all-natural cough suppressant. Bone broth and honey also calm the coughing instinct and soothe a scratchy throat. And both thyme and honey have antibacterial properties to help you fight possible causes of that cough.

Makes 2 servings

Ingredients

6 cups water
2 handfuls fresh thyme leaves
1 cup Immune System Powerhouse
   Bone Broth (page 61) or
   Basic Chicken Bone Broth (page 41)
2 tablespoons raw honey

Instructions

1. Bring the water to a boil in a pot and then add the thyme leaves. Lower the heat and simmer for 20 minutes, or until the liquid is reduced by half.
2. Remove from the heat, add the broth and honey, and stir until the honey dissolves. Strain out the thyme leaves.

Probiotic Tonic

Combine probiotics with the gut-healing properties of bone broth, and you have a recipe for happiness inside. Be sure to follow the directions for broth temperature and to follow the steps in order, waiting to add the probiotics last. Adding probiotics to hot liquid will kill the beneficial bacteria and rob you of all the benefits.

Makes 2 servings

Ingredients
1 cup Digestive Double-Team
   Bone Broth (page 59) or
   Mixed Poultry Bone Broth (page 44)
2 teaspoons yellow miso paste
1 cup liquid probiotics: unflavored kefir,
   unflavored kombucha, or
   fermented vegetable juice

Instructions
1. Heat the broth in a saucepan over low heat until just warm.
2. Remove from the heat and whisk in the miso paste.
3. Add the liquid probiotic of your choice and stir briefly.

Scotch Brocktail

Bone broth cocktails (aka brocktails or stocktails) have popped up on the menus of many fashionable restaurants. This recipe is a super-simple way to try the trend. If your bone broth is already at room temperature, you can skip the first step. To switch it up, swap vodka or rum for the Scotch.

Makes 2 servings

Ingredients
½ cup Basic Beef Bone Broth (page 39)
  or Basic Lamb Bone Broth (page 42)
2 ounces Scotch
Dash of salt

Instructions
1. Heat the bone broth in a small saucepan until it comes to room temperature and is no longer gelled.
2. Pour the broth and Scotch into glasses and mix together with a dash of salt. Serve warm, at room temperature, or on ice.

Bone Broth Mary

Perhaps the most common savory cocktail in existence, a Bloody Mary with bone broth added should be a comfortable step into the brocktail party. The drink by nature is salty and full of umami flavor due to Worcestershire sauce, making the addition of a dark bone broth a natural one.

Makes 2 servings

Ingredients
½ cup Basic Lamb Bone Broth (page 42)
½ cup vodka
½ cup tomato juice
Juice of 1 lemon
2–4 dashes hot sauce
2 dashes Worcestershire sauce
1 teaspoon grated horseradish root (optional)
½ teaspoon celery salt
Pepper, to taste
Garnish: celery stalk, beef jerky, slice of bacon,
     grape tomato, or pickled vegetable of choice

Instructions
1. Heat the bone broth in a small saucepan until it comes to room temperature and is no longer gelled.
2. Combine all the ingredients in a shaker with ice and shake until well combined. Serve over ice in highball glasses with the garnish of your choice.

After-Dinner Digestif

Bone broth adds a meaty flavor and richness to a simple after-dinner sherry, making you feel good in more ways than one! For extra pizzazz and a bit of color, garnish with cilantro—it's perfect for after dinner, as it's known for relieving indigestion and bloating.

Makes 2 servings

Ingredients

1 cup Basic Chicken Bone Broth (page 41)
   or Basic Beef Bone Broth (page 39)
1 cup sherry

Instructions

1. Heat the broth in a saucepan until very warm.
2. Pour into two glasses and mix in the sherry.

Hot Broth Toddy

Cool evening or slight head cold bringing you down? This evening relaxer will warm you up with whiskey, broth, and spices. As classic food remedies, chicken broth and honey relieve any cold symptoms you might be suffering, while cinnamon and cloves are known for fighting infection.

Makes 2 servings

Ingredients
¼ cup Basic Chicken Bone Broth (page 41)
3 ounces whiskey
2 teaspoons honey
4 whole cloves
2 cinnamon sticks
2 lemon slices
2 pinches ground nutmeg

Instructions
1. Bring the broth to a boil in a small saucepan.
2. Pour the broth, whiskey, and honey into two mugs.
3. Add the cloves, cinnamon sticks, and lemon slices and let stand for 5 minutes. Sprinkle with the nutmeg.

Soups, Stews & Chilis

Once you have your bone broth basics down, you can use any of the bone broth recipes in the previous chapters to help make these savory soups, stews, and chilis. Each recipe included here features enough bone broth to get at least half of a serving but usually more. Best of all, you only need your Instant Pot to get amazing results in a short time with very little effort! Remember: When using premade bone broth as part of a recipe, you may need to let the broth come to room temperature or heat it a little until it is no longer gelled. Plan ahead as needed for that simple step.

Chicken Bone Broth Noodle Soup

Whether you use the Basic Chicken Bone Broth or the Vegetable & Chicken Bone Broth, you'll have the perfect bowl of comfort food with this recipe. It's simple to prepare, which is especially good if you're feeling under the weather.

Makes 6 servings

Ingredients

2 teaspoons olive oil

3 medium carrots, peeled and thinly sliced

2 medium celery ribs, thinly sliced

1 small onion, diced

4–5 cups Basic Chicken Bone Broth (page 41) or Vegetable & Chicken Bone Broth (page 49)

1 pound boneless, skinless chicken thighs and/or breasts, cut into bite-size pieces

3 tablespoons minced fresh parsley

½ teaspoon dried thyme

¼ teaspoon salt

¼ teaspoon pepper

6 ounces dried noodles

TIP
Want to use precooked chicken instead? Cut it into bite-size pieces and stir it in later with the noodles.

Instructions

1. Add the oil to the Instant Pot and press Sauté. When hot, stir in the carrots, celery, and onion and sauté for 3 minutes, or until the carrots are tender.
2. Stir in the broth, chicken, parsley, thyme, salt, and pepper.
3. Lock the lid and make sure the valve is sealed. Select Manual/High Pressure and adjust the time to 12 minutes.
4. When the cook time is complete, turn off the Instant Pot and let the pressure release naturally for 5 to 10 minutes before turning the valve to venting. Then, remove the lid.
5. Set the pressure cooker to Sauté. Heat until the soup comes to a simmer. Stir in the noodles, adding more broth if needed. Cook for 8 to 10 minutes, or until the noodles are tender, stirring frequently.

Super Greens Soup

Green smoothies have been all the rage for years now. Take that love to a soup bowl by gently cooking your greens in bone broth. You can't go wrong no matter which hearty greens you choose, as they all contain powerful nutrients that fuel good health.

Makes 6–8 servings

Ingredients

6 cups Basic Beef Bone Broth (page 39)
3–4 cups chopped leafy greens, such as kale,
    collard, spinach, chard, mustard, or dandelion
¾ teaspoon salt
1 tablespoon unsalted butter
½ cup chopped fresh parsley
Juice of ½ lemon

TIP
You can also place this mix in the blender and puree it. Then refrigerate and serve as a smoothie.

Instructions

1. Add the broth to the Instant Pot. Lock the lid and make sure the valve is sealed. Select Manual/High Pressure and adjust the time to 5 minutes.
2. When the cook time is complete, turn off the Instant Pot and let the pressure release naturally for 5 to 10 minutes before turning the valve to venting. Then, remove the lid.
3. Set the pressure cooker to Sauté. Add the greens and salt, and cook uncovered until the greens have wilted.
4. Stir in the butter, parsley, and lemon juice and serve.

Chinese Pork & Noodle Soup

This soup will taste better than any you can buy from a restaurant, especially if you have Chinese five-spice powder, which includes cinnamon, cloves, toasted fennel, star anise, and Szechuan peppercorns. You can add more Chinese five-spice powder if you want your dish a little spicier.

Makes 4 servings

Ingredients

1 pound pork tenderloin, cut into bite-size pieces

1 teaspoon Chinese five-spice powder

Salt, to taste

2 tablespoons peeled, minced ginger

3 cloves garlic, minced

1 cup soy sauce

¼ cup dark brown sugar

2 tablespoons sesame oil

4 cups Basic Chicken Bone Broth (page 41)

6 ounces dried udon noodles

1½ cups sliced shiitake mushrooms

2 cups coarsely chopped bok choy, tough stems discarded

Sliced radishes, for garnish (optional)

Sliced green onion, for garnish (optional)

Instructions

1. Add the pork, Chinese five-spice powder, salt, ginger, garlic, soy sauce, sugar, sesame oil, and broth to the Instant Pot. Stir to combine.
2. Lock the lid and make sure the valve is sealed. Select Manual/High Pressure and adjust the time to 45 minutes.
3. Meanwhile, cook the udon noodles according to the package directions.
4. When the cook time is complete, turn off the Instant Pot and let the pressure release naturally for 5 to 10 minutes before turning the valve to venting. Then, remove the lid.
5. Add the mushrooms and bok choy. Lock the lid and make sure the valve is sealed. Select Manual/High Pressure and adjust the time to 1 minute. Release the pressure manually and remove the lid.
6. Place the noodles in serving bowls and top with the soup along with the radishes and/or green onion if using.

Slimmed-Down Corn Chowder

Traditional comfort foods can get healthier when made with bone broth and packed with vegetables. A simple swap of milk for heavy cream trims down this recipe, but feel free to go to light cream for a more decadent texture and taste. It all comes together so quickly in the Instant Pot!

Makes 4 servings

Ingredients

3 cups Basic Chicken Bone Broth (page 41)

2 cups frozen or fresh corn kernels

1 cup diced potato

1 cup chopped onion

1 cup chopped bell pepper

3 slices bacon, cooked and chopped, plus extra
    for serving

4 cloves garlic, minced

1 teaspoon salt

1 teaspoon black pepper

½ teaspoon dried thyme

½ teaspoon ground nutmeg

½ cup milk

2 tablespoons chopped fresh parsley leaves, for garnish

TIP

If you have a little more time on your hands, you can cook the bacon in the Instant Pot first. Simply press the Sauté button, wait 2 minutes for the pot to warm up, and add the bacon. Cook until crispy and, without draining the bacon fat, add the next ingredients.

Instructions

1. In the Instant Pot, combine the broth, corn, potato, onion, pepper, bacon, garlic, salt, pepper, and thyme. Stir to combine. Lock the lid and make sure the valve is sealed. Select Manual/High Pressure and adjust the time to 10 minutes.

2. When the cook time is complete, turn off the Instant Pot and let the pressure release naturally for 5 to 10 minutes before turning the valve to venting. Then, remove the lid.

3. Puree some of the soup with an immersion blender, but leave some of the corn and potatoes intact. Add the nutmeg and milk and stir. Serve garnished with the parsley and extra bacon pieces.

Zuppa Toscana

Italian for "Tuscan soup," zuppa Toscana has many variations but often includes kale, potatoes, and sausage. This version tastes even better than the kind you can find at a certain chain of family Italian restaurants. More good news: it cooks up quickly so you can enjoy it any time!

Makes 4 servings

Ingredients

1 tablespoon olive oil
1 pound ground Italian sausage
1 large onion, quartered
3 cloves garlic, minced
1 tablespoon dried oregano
1 teaspoon crushed red pepper flakes
Salt and pepper, to taste
1½ pounds russet potatoes, cut into ½-inch cubes
6 cups Basic Chicken Bone Broth (page 41)
4 cups chopped kale
1 cup full-fat coconut milk

Instructions

1. Add the oil to the Instant Pot, and then press Sauté. When hot, add the sausage and cook for 5 minutes.
2. Add the onion and garlic and cook for 2 minutes.
3. Add the oregano, red pepper flakes, salt, and pepper and cook for 1 minute.
4. Add the potatoes and broth. Lock the lid and make sure the valve is sealed. Select Manual/High Pressure and adjust the time to 5 minutes.
5. When the cook time is complete, turn off the Instant Pot and let the pressure release naturally for 5 to 10 minutes before turning the valve to venting. Then, remove the lid.
6. Press the Sauté setting again, stir in the kale, and cook until wilted. Stir in the coconut milk.

Beef Chili with a Boost

Traditional beef and bean chili gets a nutrition boost when you introduce bone broth. You can easily adjust the heat in this recipe by adding the peppers of your choice—go mild or spicy, depending on your taste. Cooking it all in the Instant Pot gives you simmered-for-hours flavor in a fraction of the time.

Makes 4–6 servings

Ingredients

1½ tablespoons olive oil

1 onion, diced

4 cloves garlic, minced

1 cubanelle or green bell pepper, seeded and diced

1 poblano chile, minced

2 pounds chuck steak, cubed

3 tablespoons tomato paste

3 tablespoons chili powder

2 teaspoons smoked paprika

2 teaspoons dried oregano

½ teaspoon ground cumin

2½ cups Basic Beef Bone Broth (page 39)

2 (10.75-ounce) cans tomato puree

2 (15-ounce) cans black beans, drained and rinsed

¼ cup chopped fresh cilantro leaves

Salt and pepper, to taste

Shredded cheddar cheese, chopped green onion, sliced peppers, and/or sour cream, for serving (optional)

Instructions

1. Add the oil to the Instant Pot, and then press Sauté. When hot, add the onion, garlic, cubanelle pepper, and chile. Sauté for 3 minutes, or until the peppers are tender.
2. Add the beef and cook for 5 minutes, or until browned. Press cancel.
3. Add the tomato paste, chili powder, paprika, oregano, cumin, bone broth, tomato puree, and beans. Lock the lid and make sure the valve is sealed. Select Manual/High Pressure and adjust the time to 20 minutes.
4. When the cook time is complete, turn off the Instant Pot and let the pressure release naturally for 5 to 10 minutes before turning the valve to venting. Then, remove the lid. If you wish to reduce the liquid a bit, press the Sauté setting again and simmer until it reaches the desired consistency.
5. Stir in the cilantro, season with salt and pepper to taste, and serve with the toppings of your choice.

Chicken & Vegetables in Broth

Some recipes are just so versatile and hardworking that you keep them close at hand in the kitchen. This is one of those recipes! With this basic recipe you can adjust the spices, herbs, and vegetables to suit your taste. Want more of a stew? Make it as is. Want a soup? Add more broth.

Makes 4–8 servings

Ingredients

2 tablespoons olive oil
2 tablespoons Dijon mustard
1 medium onion, sliced
2 cloves garlic, minced
4 medium carrots, peeled and cut
    into 1-inch pieces
1 medium zucchini, sliced
1 cup Basic Chicken Bone Broth (page 41)
1 tablespoon tapioca flour
8 bone-in chicken pieces
1 teaspoon salt
½ teaspoon pepper
Chopped parsley, for garnish

Instructions

1. Add the oil and mustard to the Instant Pot, and press Sauté. When hot, stir in the onion, garlic, carrots, and zucchini. Cook for 3 minutes, or until the vegetables are tender.
2. Stir in the broth, tapioca flour, chicken, salt, and pepper.
3. Lock the lid and make sure the valve is sealed. Select Manual/High Pressure and adjust the time to 12 minutes.
4. When the cook time is complete, turn off the Instant Pot and let the pressure release naturally for 5 to 10 minutes before turning the valve to venting. Then, remove the lid.
5. Serve in bowls and top with the parsley.

Herbed Beef Stew

A savory beef recipe can be your best friend in the kitchen, especially when your Instant Pot speeds the simmering. When you make it with bone broth, you take it to the next level. This recipe is just as tasty if pork loin is substituted for the beef.

Makes 4 servings

Ingredients

1 tablespoon olive oil

2 pounds stew beef

3 cups Basic Beef Bone Broth (page 39)

2 tablespoons all-purpose flour

1 tablespoon Worcestershire sauce

1 tablespoon tomato paste

4 potatoes, peeled and cut into
   1-inch cubes

3 medium carrots, peeled and sliced

1 medium onion, chopped

2 cloves garlic, minced

2 teaspoons chopped fresh thyme

½ teaspoon dried rosemary

Salt and pepper, to taste

2 tablespoons chopped fresh parsley
   leaves, for garnish

Instructions

1. Add the oil to the Instant Pot, and press Sauté. When hot, add the beef in batches and cook for 5 minutes, or until browned on all sides.
2. In a medium bowl, combine the broth, flour, Worcestershire sauce, and tomato paste. Whisk well.
3. With all the beef in the pot, add the broth mixture, potatoes, carrots, onion, garlic, thyme, rosemary, salt, and pepper. Stir well.
4. Lock the lid and make sure the valve is sealed. Select the Meat/Stew function, and adjust the time to 25 minutes.
5. When the cook time is complete, turn off the Instant Pot and let the pressure release naturally for 5 to 10 minutes before turning the valve to venting. Then, remove the lid and serve garnished with the parsley.

Vietnamese Beef Pho

The secret to this traditional Vietnamese stew is what's in the bag: the ginger, cloves, star anise, and peppercorns. Infusing the broth adds an incredibly rich and delicious flavor, and having bone broth on hand makes this dish quick and easy to make.

Makes 4 servings

Ingredients

2-inch piece ginger

2 cloves

1 star anise

6 peppercorns

6 cups Basic Beef Bone Broth (page 39)

1 pound sirloin, very thinly sliced

1 tablespoon fish sauce

2 tablespoons coconut sugar

12 ounces rice noodles

Garnishes: 1 cup each of bean sprouts, cilantro leaves, mint leaves, sliced green onion, hoisin sauce, lime wedges, and/or thinly sliced Thai chile peppers

Instructions

1. In a bouquet garni bag, add the ginger, cloves, star anise, and peppercorns. Secure closed.
2. In the Instant Pot, add the broth and bouquet garni bag. Press Sauté and bring the broth to a boil. Press the – (or Less) button to lower the heat, and simmer to infuse the broth for 15 to 20 minutes.
3. Remove the bag and add the sirloin, fish sauce, and coconut sugar. Turn off the pot and stir briefly to cook the steak.
4. Prepare the noodles according to the package instructions. Add 1 cup noodles to each serving bowl and top with the soup. Garnish as desired.

Beef Barley Soup

There is lots to love about this soup—even beyond the bone broth! It features barley, a highly nutritious but often underappreciated seed. In fact, barley is a better source of dietary fiber than rice, making it a great choice for keeping blood sugar in balance. Barley is also packed with essential minerals and cooks so easily in your Instant Pot.

Makes 4 servings

Ingredients

1 tablespoon olive oil

1 pound stew meat or steak, cut into 1-inch chunks

Salt and pepper, to taste

1 onion, chopped

2 cloves garlic, minced

3 carrots, peeled and sliced

1 celery rib, thinly sliced

4 cups Basic Beef Bone Broth (page 39)

1 (14-ounce) can diced tomatoes, drained

½ cup uncooked pearl barley

2 bay leaves

1 teaspoon Worcestershire sauce

Instructions

1. Add the oil to the Instant Pot, and press Sauté. When hot, add the beef and season with salt and pepper. Cook the beef for 5 minutes, or until evenly brown on all sides, working in batches if necessary.
2. Add the remaining ingredients. Lock the lid and make sure the valve is sealed. Select Manual/High Pressure and adjust the time to 20 minutes.
3. When the cook time is complete, turn off the Instant Pot and let the pressure release naturally for 5 to 10 minutes before turning the valve to venting. Then, remove the lid.
4. If the beef is still a little tough, cook for another 5 minutes, or until the beef nearly falls apart. Remove the bay leaves and serve.

Tunisian Lamb Stew

The spices featured in this dish are staples of North African cooking and accent the flavor of the lamb very well when simmered in the Instant Pot. But if you're not a fan of lamb or it's not available to you, feel free to use cubes of beef or ground beef instead. Simply match your bone broth to the selection, and enjoy the rich flavor and nutrients it adds. For a satisfying meal, try this stew served over rice.

Makes 4 servings

Ingredients

1 tablespoon olive oil

1 large onion, chopped

1 pound lamb, cut into 1-inch cubes, or ground lamb

3 cloves garlic, minced

2 tablespoons tomato paste

3 cups Basic Lamb Bone Broth (page 42) or Basic Beef Bone Broth (page 39)

1 teaspoon ground cumin

1 teaspoon ground coriander

½ teaspoon ground ginger

½ teaspoon turmeric

¼ teaspoon cayenne pepper

¼ teaspoon ground cinnamon

Salt and pepper, to taste

1 cup canned chickpeas, drained

1 bell pepper, seeded and diced

¼ cup golden raisins

⅓ cup toasted pine nuts

Instructions

1. Add the oil to the Instant Pot, and press Sauté. When hot, add the onion and cook for 3 minutes, or until translucent. Add the lamb and garlic and cook for 3 to 4 minutes, or until the meat is evenly browned.
2. Stir in the tomato paste. Mix in the broth, cumin, coriander, ginger, turmeric, cayenne, cinnamon, salt, and pepper. Cook for 1 minute.
3. Lock the lid and make sure the valve is sealed. Select Manual/High Pressure and adjust the time to 25 minutes.
4. When the cook time is complete, turn off the Instant Pot and let the pressure release naturally for 5 to 10 minutes before turning the valve to venting. Then, remove the lid and add the chickpeas and pepper. Return to Sauté, and cook for 5 minutes.
5. Top with the raisins and pine nuts.

Butternut Squash Soup

This chilly-night favorite is smooth, creamy, and just a little bit sweet. How quickly it cooks in your Instant Pot is also pretty sweet! If you need to speed the preparation, look for pre-chopped butternut squash, available in the refrigerated produce section of many grocery stores.

Makes 4–6 servings

Ingredients

2 tablespoons olive oil
1 onion, chopped
6 cups peeled and cubed butternut squash
3 cups Basic Chicken Bone Broth (page 41)
2 teaspoons chopped fresh thyme leaves
Pinch of cayenne pepper
Pinch of ground nutmeg
Salt, to taste
½ cup heavy cream

Instructions

1. Add the oil to the Instant Pot, and press Sauté. When hot, add the onion and cook for 3 minutes, or until translucent.
2. Add the squash, broth, thyme, cayenne, nutmeg, and salt.
3. Lock the lid and make sure the valve is sealed. Select Manual/High Pressure and adjust the time to 5 minutes.
4. When the cook time is complete, turn off the Instant Pot and let the pressure release naturally for 5 to 10 minutes before turning the valve to venting. Then, remove the lid. The squash should easily break apart at this point. Stir in the cream.
5. Puree the soup with an immersion blender or in a blender.

Minestrone Soup

This soup comes together so quickly using the Instant Pot that perhaps we should call it Minute-strone! You can make substitutions for any vegetables you don't have available; just keep the overall amounts the same. For some extra greens, add a few cups of chopped kale or spinach when you're finished cooking but the soup is still in the pot.

Makes 4 servings

Ingredients

2 tablespoons olive oil

3 cloves garlic, minced

1 onion, diced

2 carrots, peeled and diced

2 celery ribs, diced

4 cups Basic Chicken Bone Broth
   (page 41)

1 (28-ounce) can diced tomatoes

1 (15.5-ounce) can cannellini or red
   kidney beans, drained and rinsed

1½ cups uncooked elbow macaroni or
   other small pasta

1 cup green beans

1 medium zucchini, sliced

2 teaspoons dried basil

2 teaspoons dried oregano

½ teaspoon fennel seeds

1 bay leaf

Salt and pepper, to taste

⅓ cup freshly grated Parmesan,
   for garnish

2 tablespoons chopped fresh parsley
   leaves, for garnish

⅓ cup shredded kale, for garnish

Instructions

1. Add the oil to the Instant Pot, and press Sauté. When hot, add the garlic, onion, carrots, and celery. Cook, stirring occasionally, for 3 minutes, or until the carrots are tender.

2. Stir in the broth, tomatoes, beans, pasta, green beans, zucchini, basil, oregano, fennel, bay leaf, salt, and pepper.

3. Lock the lid and make sure the valve is sealed. Select Manual/High Pressure and adjust the time to 5 minutes.

4. When the cook time is complete, turn off the Instant Pot and let the pressure release naturally for 5 to 10 minutes before turning the valve to venting. Then, remove the lid.

5. Serve garnished with the Parmesan cheese, parsley, and/or shredded kale.

Chicken Tortilla Soup

Store-bought salsa not only makes this a super-easy soup to put together, but you can also instantly adjust the heat by purchasing mild, medium, or hot salsa. This recipe doesn't include beans, but you can add a 15-ounce can of drained and rinsed black beans before you lock the lid, if you like. Top each bowl with a dollop of sour cream and a slice of lime.

Makes 4 servings

Ingredients

4 boneless, skinless chicken thighs, cut into bite-size pieces

2 cups Basic Chicken Bone Broth (page 41)

1 medium onion, chopped

1 cup mild, medium, or hot salsa

1 teaspoon ground cumin

½ teaspoon chili powder

Salt and pepper, to taste

1 cup frozen corn, thawed

½ cup chopped fresh cilantro

4 corn tortillas, sliced into strips

Instructions

1. Add the chicken, broth, onion, salsa, cumin, chili powder, salt, and pepper to the Instant Pot. Stir to combine.
2. Lock the lid and make sure the valve is sealed. Select Manual/High Pressure and adjust the time to 5 minutes.
3. When the cook time is complete, turn off the Instant Pot and let the pressure release naturally for 5 to 10 minutes before turning the valve to venting. Then, remove the lid.
4. Stir in the corn and cilantro. Serve topped with the tortillas.

Lentil Soup

Lentil soups are so satisfying without ever feeling heavy. Packed with nutrients, this is the ultimate, throw-all-the-ingredients-in-the-pot-and-forget-about-it recipe. However, feel free to start off by sautéing the veggies a little first if you want to punch up the flavor.

Makes 4 servings

Ingredients

4 cups Basic Chicken Bone Broth (page 41)
1½ cups dried green lentils
1 (14.5-ounce) can diced tomatoes, drained
2 celery ribs, chopped
3 cloves garlic, minced
1 large onion, chopped
1 medium carrot, peeled and chopped
2 teaspoons chopped fresh thyme
1 teaspoon Italian seasoning
Salt and pepper, to taste
4 cups spinach
Freshly grated Parmesan

Instructions

1. Add the broth, lentils, tomatoes, celery, garlic, onion, carrot, thyme, Italian seasoning, salt, and pepper to the Instant Pot.
2. Lock the lid and make sure the valve is sealed. Select Manual/High Pressure and adjust the time to 18 minutes.
3. When the cook time is complete, turn off the Instant Pot and let the pressure release naturally for 5 to 10 minutes before turning the valve to venting. Then, remove the lid and stir in the spinach. Serve topped with grated Parmesan.

Sweet Potato Chili with Turkey

Why wait for the holidays to mix up this instant family classic that combines Thanksgiving favorites with Southwest seasonings and black beans? You'll want to eat this year-round—and there's no reason not to when it serves up so much nutrition and doesn't heat up your kitchen because you're using the Instant Pot! It's a great way to use your premade bone broth.

Makes 6 servings

Ingredients

1 tablespoon olive oil
1 pound ground turkey
1 small onion, diced
4 cups Thanksgiving Turkey Bone Broth (page 47)
   or Basic Chicken Bone Broth (page 41)
1 (15.5-ounce) can black beans, drained and rinsed
2 sweet potatoes, peeled and cut into 1-inch pieces
2 cloves garlic, minced
2 tablespoons chili powder
1 teaspoon ground cumin
Salt, to taste
Chopped fresh cilantro, for garnish
Sour cream, for garnish

Instructions

1. Add the oil to the Instant Pot, and press Sauté. When hot, add the turkey and onion. Cook until the turkey is no longer pink.
2. Stir in the broth, beans, sweet potatoes, garlic, chili powder, cumin, and salt.
3. Lock the lid and make sure the valve is sealed. Select Manual/High Pressure and adjust the time to 5 minutes.
4. When the cook time is complete, turn off the Instant Pot and let the pressure release naturally for 5 to 10 minutes before turning the valve to venting. Then, remove the lid and stir before serving topped with cilantro and sour cream.

Egg Drop Soup

This classic Asian soup is a cinch to make with the Instant Pot and benefits in the taste and nutrition departments from chicken bone broth. If you want some greens, add 1 to 2 cups of spinach (or even kale) right after adding the cornstarch. Let the greens wilt before serving. Serve alone or over noodles.

Ingredients
4 cups Basic Chicken Bone Broth
    (page 41)
1 teaspoon sesame oil
1 teaspoon ground ginger
½ teaspoon garlic powder
Salt and pepper, to taste
½ cup chopped green onion,
    plus extra for serving
¼ teaspoon turmeric
2 tablespoons cornstarch
2 tablespoons water
2 large eggs, beaten

Instructions
1. Add the broth, sesame oil, ginger, garlic powder, salt, and pepper to the Instant Pot. Lock the lid and make sure the valve is sealed.
2. Select Manual/High Pressure and adjust the time to 3 minutes. When the cook time is complete, turn off the Instant Pot and do a quick release.
3. Press the Sauté button, and add the green onion and turmeric. In a small bowl, mix together the cornstarch and water. Add this mixture to the pot and cook for 1 minute, or until the soup begins to bubble.
4. Turn off the pot and add the eggs. Mix well until the egg forms ribbons and is cooked through.

Bean Soup with Sausage & Kale

If you want to use dried cannellini beans, first soak them in cool water overnight. Drain, and then cook the soaked beans along with 4 cups of water in the Instant Pot on Manual/High Pressure for 25 minutes.

Makes 4 servings

Ingredients

2 tablespoons olive oil
1 pound ground Italian sausage
1 onion, chopped
1 carrot, peeled and chopped
1 celery rib, chopped
2 cloves garlic, minced
1 teaspoon dried rosemary
4 cups Basic Chicken Bone Broth
   (page 41)
2 (14-ounce) cans cannellini beans,
   drained and rinsed
1 large bunch kale, stemmed
   and chopped
Salt and pepper, to taste

Instructions

1. Add the oil to the Instant Pot, and press Sauté. When hot, add the sausage and cook for 3 minutes, or until evenly browned.
2. Add the onion, carrot, celery, garlic, and rosemary. Cook for 2 minutes, stirring frequently.
3. Add the broth, beans, and kale, and stir until combined.
4. Lock the lid and make sure the valve is sealed. Select Manual/High Pressure and adjust the time to 8 minutes.
5. When the cook time is complete, turn off the Instant Pot, manually release the pressure, remove the lid, and season to taste with salt and pepper.

Spicy Sweet Potato Soup

This delicious soup gets its kick from harissa, a Tunisian hot chile pepper paste. These days, you can find it at just about any grocery store. If you need to, you can use tomato paste instead, but be sure to make up for the lack of heat with some crushed red pepper flakes.

Makes 4 servings

Ingredients

1 tablespoon olive oil
1 onion, diced
2 cloves garlic, minced
4 cups Basic Chicken Bone Broth (page 41)
2–3 sweet potatoes, peeled and
    cut into 1-inch pieces
1 (15.5-ounce) can chickpeas,
    drained and rinsed
2 tablespoons harissa paste
2 teaspoons ground cumin
Salt and pepper, to taste
Crushed red pepper flakes, to taste
Ground cinnamon, to taste
Fresh cilantro leaves, for garnish

Instructions

1. Add the oil to the Instant Pot, and press Sauté. When hot, add the onion and garlic and cook for 3 minutes, or until the onion is translucent.
2. Add the broth, sweet potatoes, chickpeas, harissa paste, cumin, salt, pepper, red pepper flakes, and cinnamon. Lock the lid and make sure the valve is sealed. Select Manual/High Pressure and adjust the time to 3 minutes.
3. When the cook time is complete, turn off the Instant Pot and let the pressure release naturally for 5 to 10 minutes before turning the valve to venting. Then, remove the lid.
4. Adjust the seasonings, garnish with cilantro, and serve.

Tom Kha Gai

This Thai-style coconut chicken soup is sweet with just the right amount of kick. The taste will make you feel like you're dining at a fine Thai restaurant, although this version will be ready quicker than the waiter coming back with your drink order.

Makes 4 servings

Ingredients

1 pound chicken breast, cut into 1-inch slices

3 cups Basic Chicken Bone Broth (page 41)

1 (14-ounce) can unsweetened coconut milk

Juice from 1 lime

2 tablespoons fish sauce

1 tablespoon sesame oil

1 cup sliced cremini mushrooms

6 to 8 thin slices fresh ginger

1 bunch green onions, sliced

1 tablespoon minced fresh lemongrass

½ tablespoon sugar

¼ teaspoon crushed red pepper flakes

1 tablespoon fresh basil

Salt, to taste

Chopped fresh cilantro, for garnish

Hot sauce, for garnish

Instructions

1. Add all the ingredients except for the garnishes to the Instant Pot. Stir well.
2. Lock the lid and make sure the valve is sealed. Select Manual/High Pressure and adjust the time to 6 minutes.
3. When the cook time is complete, turn off the Instant Pot and turn the valve to venting for quick pressure release. Then, remove the lid, and top with the cilantro and hot sauce before serving.

Split Pea Soup

This soup dates back to the ancient Romans, although it took them a lot longer to cook it than it will you—especially with premade bone broth and your Instant Pot at hand. If you want, use bacon instead of ham. When choosing split peas, note that the yellow split peas are a little sweeter than green split peas.

Makes 4 servings

Ingredients
2 tablespoons olive oil
2 carrots, peeled and coarsely chopped
2 celery ribs, sliced
1 large onion, coarsely chopped
3 cloves garlic, minced
Salt and pepper, to taste
5 cups Basic Chicken Bone Broth (page 41)
1½ cups dried yellow split peas
1 cup diced ham
1 tablespoon chopped fresh thyme
1 tablespoon fresh lemon juice, or to taste

Instructions
1. Add the oil to the Instant Pot, and press Sauté. When hot, add the carrots, celery, onion, and garlic. Season with salt and pepper and cook for 5 minutes while stirring, or until the veggies are softened.
2. Add the broth, split peas, ham, and thyme. Lock the lid and make sure the valve is sealed. Select Manual/High Pressure and adjust the time to 12 minutes.
3. When the cook time is complete, turn off the Instant Pot and let the pressure release naturally for 5 to 10 minutes before turning the valve to venting. Then, remove the lid.
4. Stir in the lemon juice and season to taste.

Chickpea & Chorizo Soup

Hailing from Spain, chorizo is pork seasoned with garlic, smoked paprika, and salt. It can be sweet or spicy; either works in this classic soup. If you decide to use canned chickpeas, reduce the cook time to 12 minutes, and don't add the chickpeas until after you've removed the lid. Give the beans a few minutes to heat up before serving.

Makes 4 servings

Ingredients
1 tablespoon olive oil
1 onion, chopped
5 cloves garlic, minced
6 ounces Spanish chorizo, sliced
5 cups Basic Chicken Bone Broth (page 41)
1½ cups dried chickpeas
2 bay leaves
4 cups chopped escarole
1 tablespoon sherry vinegar
Salt and pepper, to taste
¼ teaspoon crushed red pepper flakes

Instructions
1. Add the oil to the Instant Pot, and press Sauté. When hot, add the onion and cook for 3 minutes, or until translucent.
2. Add the garlic and chorizo and cook, stirring frequently, for 3 minutes.
3. Add the broth, chickpeas, and bay leaves; stir.
4. Lock the lid and make sure the valve is sealed. Select Manual/High Pressure and adjust the time to 60 minutes.
5. When the cook time is complete, turn off the Instant Pot and let the pressure release naturally for 5 to 10 minutes before turning the valve to venting. Then, remove the lid.
6. Remove the bay leaves, add the escarole, sherry vinegar, salt, pepper, and red pepper flakes. Stir until the escarole wilts, and then serve.

Lamb Bone Broth Borscht

Known for its deep red color, borscht is an Eastern European soup that usually features beets, cabbage, and beef. This version switches out the beef for lamb but retains the other classic ingredients. Feel free to add the traditional dollop of sour cream if you wish, although this borscht tastes great without it.

Makes 6 servings

Ingredients

1 tablespoon olive oil
1 pound lamb, cut into 1-inch pieces
2 cloves garlic, minced
1 onion, diced
6 cups Basic Lamb Bone Broth (page 42)
    or Basic Beef Bone Broth (page 39)
1 pound red beets, peeled and diced
1 head cabbage, cored and chopped
1 (15-ounce) can diced tomatoes, drained
¼ cup red wine vinegar
Salt and pepper, to taste
Chopped fresh parsley, for garnish

Instructions

1. Add the oil to the Instant Pot, and press Sauté. When hot, add the lamb and cook for 3 minutes, or until evenly browned.
2. Add the garlic and onion and cook for 3 minutes, or until the onion is translucent.
3. Add the broth, beets, cabbage, tomatoes, and red wine vinegar.
4. Lock the lid and make sure the valve is sealed. Select Manual/High Pressure and adjust the time to 10 minutes.
5. When the cook time is complete, turn off the Instant Pot and let the pressure release naturally for 5 to 10 minutes before turning the valve to venting. Then, remove the lid.
6. Season with salt and pepper and top with chopped parsley.

Cioppino

This seafood stew easily incorporates bone broth and can be made with just about any type of seafood, including whitefish, shrimp, scallops, mussels, and calamari. When entertaining, it's a dish sure to impress guests, even though your Instant Pot makes it simple to prepare.

Makes 4 servings

Ingredients

3 tablespoons olive oil

1 large fennel bulb, trimmed and thinly sliced

1 onion, diced

3 shallots, chopped

Salt, to taste

3 cloves garlic, minced

1 teaspoon crushed red pepper flakes, plus more for garnish

1 (14.5-ounce) can diced tomatoes in juice

2 cups Basic Chicken Bone Broth (page 41) or Basic Fish Bone Broth (page 43)

1 tablespoon tomato paste

1 teaspoon dried oregano

2 bay leaves

4 cups mixed seafood

2 tablespoons fresh lemon juice

Chopped fresh parsley, for garnish

Instructions

1. Add the oil to the Instant Pot, and press Sauté. When hot, add the fennel, onion, shallots, and salt. Cook for 3 minutes, or until the onion is translucent.
2. Add the garlic and red pepper flakes and cook for 2 minutes.
3. Stir in the tomatoes, broth, tomato paste, oregano, and bay leaves. Lock the lid and make sure the valve is sealed. Select Manual/High Pressure and adjust the time to 15 minutes.
4. When the cook time is complete, turn off the Instant Pot and let the pressure release naturally for 5 to 10 minutes before turning the valve to venting. Then, remove the lid.
5. Return to Sauté and bring the soup to a boil. Add the seafood and cook for 4 minutes, or until the seafood is cooked through. Stir in the lemon juice, discard the bay leaves, and serve topped with parsley.

Sides & Sauces

These recipes find those little places where you can add bone broth that will make a big difference in taste and in your health. You can sneak bone broth into a homemade ketchup or sauce, use it to make rice and quinoa, and cook up some savory vegetables . . . all in the Instant Pot! Remember: When using bone broth as part of a recipe, you may need to let it come to room temperature or heat it a little until it is no longer gelled.

Bacon Green Beans

Just a little bacon and bone broth jazz up otherwise basic green beans to bring everyone to the table. Precooked bacon saves you time in the dinner rush. But, you can also cook the bacon in the Instant Pot for 5 minutes first and then sauté the onion in the bacon drippings. Experiment with other vegetables, such as okra, artichokes, kale, Brussels sprouts, and more.

Makes 6 servings

Ingredients
1 tablespoon olive oil
½ onion, diced
5 slices bacon, cooked and diced
6 cups green beans, cut in half
¼ cup Basic Chicken Bone Broth (page 41)
    or Basic Beef Bone Broth (page 39)
Salt and pepper, to taste

Instructions
1. Add the oil to the Instant Pot, and press Sauté. When hot, add the onion. Cook for 3 minutes, or until translucent.
2. Add the bacon, green beans, and broth. Lock the lid and make sure the valve is sealed. Select Manual/High Pressure and adjust the time to 4 minutes.
3. When the cook time is complete, turn off the Instant Pot and release the pressure by turning the valve to venting. Then, remove the lid, season with salt and pepper, and serve.

Collards & Beans

This classic side dish of the American South comes out of the Instant Pot perfectly creamy and delicious. You can alter this recipe by using sausage or bacon instead of the ham or by adding tomatoes and even some zucchini.

Makes 4 servings

Ingredients
4 cups coarsely chopped collard greens
2 smoked ham hocks
2 cups Basic Chicken Bone Broth (page 41)
1 cup dried black-eyed peas
6 cloves garlic, chopped
1 onion, chopped
Salt and pepper, to taste
2 teaspoons crushed red pepper flakes
2 bay leaves
1 teaspoon dried thyme
2 tablespoons apple cider vinegar
1 teaspoon hot sauce
1 teaspoon liquid smoke

Instructions
1. Add the collard greens, ham hocks, broth, black-eyed peas, garlic, onion, salt, pepper, red pepper flakes, bay leaves, and thyme to the Instant Pot.
2. Lock the lid and make sure the valve is sealed. Select Manual/High Pressure and adjust the time to 10 minutes.
3. When the cook time is complete, turn off the Instant Pot and let the pressure release naturally for 5 to 10 minutes before turning the valve to venting. Then, remove the lid.
4. Take out the ham hocks with a slotted spoon. Remove the skin and fat and discard.
5. Shred the ham and stir it back into the beans and greens. Stir in the vinegar, hot sauce, and liquid smoke. Adjust the seasonings, discard the bay leaves, and serve alone or over rice.

Sweet Potato & Apple Mash

Get ready for flavor reminiscent of a delicious dish the gourmet cook in your family might bring to Thanksgiving dinner! The combination of sweet potatoes and apples with chicken bone broth is heavenly. Fortunately, it's also so simple to whip up in the Instant Pot.

Makes 4 servings

Ingredients

2 tablespoons unsalted butter
2 medium sweet potatoes, peeled
    and cut into ½-inch cubes
2 large Granny Smith or Fuji apples,
    cored and cut into ½-inch cubes
1½ cups Basic Chicken Bone Broth
    (page 41)
1 teaspoon ground cinnamon
¾ teaspoon salt

Instructions

1. Add the butter to the Instant Pot, and press Sauté. When melted, add the sweet potatoes and cook for 5 minutes, or until lightly golden.
2. Add the apples, broth, cinnamon, and salt. Lock the lid and make sure the valve is sealed. Select Manual/High Pressure and adjust the time to 7 minutes.
3. When the cook time is complete, turn off the Instant Pot and let the pressure release naturally for 5 to 10 minutes before turning the valve to venting. Then, remove the lid.
4. With a potato masher, mash the potatoes and apples before serving.

Balsamic Brussels Sprouts with Bacon

If you cringe at the thought of Brussels sprouts, you've never tasted them like this! Once you try this quick side dish, it will become your new go-to for holiday get-togethers or for whenever you want a tasty veggie dish with dinner.

Makes 4 servings

Ingredients
2 slices bacon, chopped
1½ pounds Brussels sprouts, trimmed
½ onion, thinly sliced
1 cup Basic Chicken Bone Broth (page 41)
¼ cup shredded Parmesan cheese
2 tablespoons balsamic vinegar

Instructions
1. Press the Sauté button on your Instant Pot, and when hot, add the bacon. Cook, stirring frequently, for 3 minutes, or until browned.
2. Transfer the bacon, using a slotted spoon or tongs, to a plate covered in a paper towel to drain.
3. Add the Brussels sprouts and onion to the pot and cook, stirring occasionally, for 5 minutes, or until browned.
4. Stir in the broth. Lock the lid and make sure the valve is sealed. Select Manual/High Pressure and adjust the time to 5 minutes.
5. When the cook time is complete, turn off the Instant Pot and let the pressure release naturally for 5 to 10 minutes before turning the valve to venting. Then, remove the lid.
6. Place the sprouts in a bowl and toss with the Parmesan, bacon, and balsamic vinegar.

Bone Broth Rice

A pot of perfectly fluffy rice goes so far! Complete any meal quickly with this simple Instant Pot recipe for amazing rice every time you make it—without feeling chained to the stovetop.

Makes 6 servings

Ingredients
2 cups rice, rinsed
2 cups Basic Chicken Bone Broth (page 41)
   or any bone broth of your choice
1 tablespoon olive oil
½ teaspoon salt

Instructions
1. Add the rice, broth, olive oil, and salt to the Instant Pot.
2. Lock the lid and make sure the valve is sealed. Select the Rice button or press Manual/High Pressure and adjust the time to 5 minutes.
3. When the cook time is complete, turn off the Instant Pot and let the pressure release naturally for 5 to 10 minutes before turning the valve to venting. Then, remove the lid, fluff with a fork, and serve.

Cilantro Lime Rice

This fast and flavorful recipe will liven up your tacos and burritos instantly. In fact, it's better than the rice found in that popular burrito chain—and it works in bone broth for a nutrition boost!

Makes 4 servings

Ingredients
2 cups Basic Chicken Bone Broth (page 41)
1 cup long-grain rice, rinsed
2 cloves garlic, minced
1 tablespoon olive oil
½ cup fresh cilantro leaves
Juice of ½ lime
Salt, to taste
Lime wedges, for serving

Instructions
1. Add the broth and rice to the Instant Pot. Stir to combine.
2. Lock the lid and make sure the valve is sealed. Select Manual/High Pressure and adjust the time to 3 minutes.
3. When the cook time is complete, turn off the Instant Pot and let the pressure release naturally for 5 to 10 minutes before turning the valve to venting. Then, remove the lid.
4. Add the garlic, olive oil, cilantro, and lime juice to a food processor. Pulse until well blended.
5. Transfer the rice to a bowl and add the cilantro mixture. Mix well. Season with salt and serve with lime wedges.

Basmati Rice Pilaf

This aromatic pilaf is a great addition to any meal when you need something more than plain white rice. The best news: It only takes a few minutes more than your basic rice recipe when you use your Instant Pot.

Makes 4 servings

Ingredients
2 tablespoons unsalted butter
½ onion, diced
1 cup basmati rice, rinsed
2 cups Basic Chicken Bone Broth (page 41)

Instructions
1. Add the butter to the Instant Pot, and press Sauté. When melted, add the onion and cook, stirring frequently, for 3 minutes, or until translucent.
2. Add the rice and cook for 2 minutes, stirring well.
3. Add the broth. Lock the lid and make sure the valve is sealed. Select Manual/ High Pressure and adjust the time to 3 minutes.
4. When the cook time is complete, turn off the Instant Pot and let the pressure release naturally for 5 to 10 minutes before turning the valve to venting. Then, remove the lid and serve.

Braised Carrots & Kale

Here's a great way to get your vegetables and enjoy a helping of bone broth using the Instant Pot. Gently sautéed and then stewed in the pot, the carrots and kale come out tender and delicious.

Makes 4 servings

Ingredients
1 tablespoon olive oil
1 onion, sliced
3 carrots, peeled and sliced
10 ounces kale, roughly chopped
5 cloves garlic, chopped
½ cup Basic Chicken Bone Broth (page 41)
Salt and pepper, to taste
Balsamic vinegar, to taste
¼ teaspoon crushed red pepper flakes (optional)

Instructions
1. Add the oil to the Instant Pot, and press Sauté. When hot, add the onion and carrots. Cook for 3 to 4 minutes, or until the onion is translucent and the carrots are softened.
2. Add the kale, garlic, and broth. Lock the lid and make sure the valve is sealed. Select Manual/High Pressure and adjust the time to 7 minutes.
3. When the cook time is complete, turn off the Instant Pot and let the pressure release naturally for 5 to 10 minutes before turning the valve to venting. Then, remove the lid, stir, and adjust the seasonings with salt and pepper.
4. Drizzle on the balsamic vinegar and top with the red pepper flakes, if using.

Bone Broth Ketchup

You can even sneak bone broth into your homemade ketchup, where your family will never notice it. If you're looking for low-sugar ketchup, omit the dates.

Makes 3½ cups

Ingredients
1 (14-ounce) can diced tomatoes
1 (6-ounce) can tomato paste
½ cup Basic Chicken Bone Broth (page 41)
½ cup chopped pitted dates
2 tablespoons apple cider vinegar
1 teaspoon garlic powder
1 teaspoon onion powder
1 teaspoon salt
¼ teaspoon cayenne pepper

Instructions
1. Place all the ingredients into the Instant Pot.
2. Lock the lid and make sure the valve is sealed. Select Manual/High Pressure and adjust the time to 10 minutes.
3. When the cook time is complete, turn off the Instant Pot and let the pressure release naturally for 5 to 10 minutes before turning the valve to venting. Then, remove the lid.
4. Pour the contents into a blender and blend until smooth.
5. Pour the ketchup back into the Instant Pot, select Sauté, and cook for about 5 minutes. Stir until it thickens. Store refrigerated in mason jars for 3 to 4 weeks.

Black Beans & Quinoa with Corn

This side is perfect for stuffing burritos or tacos. Or serve over salad greens and add some chicken and avocado slices for a lunch packed with nutrition and flavor. Serve as a side dish and top with avocado, cilantro, or hot sauce.

Makes 4 servings

Ingredients

1 tablespoon olive oil

2 large jalapeños, seeded and diced

½ onion, diced

1 (10-ounce) can tomatoes and green chiles, drained

1 cup quinoa

1 cup frozen corn

1 cup Basic Chicken Bone Broth (page 41)

1 tablespoon minced garlic

1 teaspoon chili powder

½ teaspoon ground cumin

1 (14.5-ounce) can black beans, drained and rinsed

Juice from ½ lime

2 tablespoons chopped fresh cilantro

Salt and pepper, to taste

Instructions

1. Add the oil to the Instant Pot, and press Sauté. When hot, add the jalapeños and onion and cook for 3 minutes, or until the onion is translucent.
2. Stir in the tomatoes, quinoa, corn, broth, garlic, chili powder, and cumin.
3. Lock the lid and make sure the valve is sealed. Select Manual/High Pressure and adjust the time to 2 minutes.
4. When the cook time is complete, turn off the Instant Pot and let the pressure release naturally for 5 to 10 minutes before turning the valve to venting. Then, remove the lid.
5. Add the beans, lime juice, cilantro, salt, and pepper and stir to combine. Let sit for a few minutes before serving.
6. Place the lid back on the Instant Pot, select Keep Warm, and let sit for about 2 minutes to heat the beans.

Bone Broth Pasta Sauce

Everyone needs a great sauce recipe to top pasta! Adding bone broth to a traditional take on pasta sauce enriches both the taste and the nutritional profile. If you would rather use fresh tomatoes in this recipe, simply replace the can of crushed tomatoes with 10 to 12 diced medium tomatoes.

Makes 6 cups

Ingredients
2 tablespoons olive oil
1 small onion, minced
2 cups Basic Chicken Bone Broth (page 41)
   or Basic Beef Bone Broth (page 39)
1 (28-ounce) can crushed tomatoes
¼ cup tomato paste
3 cloves garlic, smashed
2 teaspoons dried oregano
1 tablespoon dried parsley
2 bay leaves
¼ teaspoon crushed red pepper flakes
1 tablespoon unsalted butter or additional olive oil
1 tablespoon honey
1 teaspoon kosher salt
½ teaspoon pepper

Instructions
1. Add the oil to the Instant Pot, and press Sauté. When hot, add the onion and cook for 3 minutes, or until translucent.
2. Add the rest of the ingredients to the pot and stir gently.
3. Lock the lid and make sure the valve is sealed. Select Manual/High Pressure and adjust the time to 25 minutes.
4. When the cook time is complete, turn off the Instant Pot and let the pressure release naturally for 5 to 10 minutes before turning the valve to venting. Then, remove the lid, and stir before serving over your favorite pasta.

Easy Cheesy Polenta

Forget all that stirring! The Instant Pot makes hands-off polenta so simple without sacrificing any of the dreamy, creamy goodness. Mix in bone broth, and it's even better. Try it served with sautéed greens or topped with tomato sauce.

Makes 6 servings

Ingredients
4 cups Basic Chicken Bone Broth (page 41)
1 cup polenta
½ cup shredded Mexican cheese blend
¼ cup light cream or half-and-half
1 tablespoon unsalted butter
Salt, to taste
Freshly grated Roquefort cheese, for garnish
Sliced tomatoes, for garnish

Instructions
1. Add the broth to the Instant Pot, and press Sauté. As soon as the broth begins to boil, slowly whisk in the polenta.
2. Lock the lid and make sure the valve is sealed. Select Manual/High Pressure and adjust the time to 7 minutes.
3. When the cook time is complete, turn off the Instant Pot and let the pressure release naturally for 5 to 10 minutes before turning the valve to venting. Then, remove the lid.
4. Whisk in the shredded Mexican cheese, cream, butter, and salt. Allow to stand for 5 minutes to thicken.
5. Serve topped with the Roquefort cheese and tomatoes.

Main Events

Get ready to taste delicious main courses that benefit from bone broth! You won't get the full serving of bone broth that you do from the soups, stews, and chilis, but these recipes will show how easy it can be to add broth where normally you might be inclined to use water. Try this little switch with some of your favorite recipes as well. Remember: When using bone broth as part of a recipe, you may have to let it come to room temperature or heat it a little until it is no longer gelled.

Beef Stroganoff

Under pressure, stew meat becomes so moist and tender that it will melt in your mouth. Once you get a taste, you won't cook beef Stroganoff without your Instant Pot ever again. If you'd rather, you can prepare the noodles separately and serve the rest of the beef Stroganoff over them.

Makes 6 servings

Ingredients

2 pounds stew meat, cut into 1-inch cubes

Salt and pepper, to taste

2 tablespoons olive oil

3 cloves garlic, minced

1 onion, diced

8 ounces button mushrooms, cut into thick slices

½ teaspoon dried thyme

3 tablespoons all-purpose flour

3 cups Basic Beef Bone Broth (page 39)

¼ cup dry sherry

2 teaspoons Worcestershire sauce

1 teaspoon Dijon mustard (lowest sodium available)

¼ teaspoon paprika

¼ teaspoon pepper (coarsely ground preferred)

6 ounces dried no-yolk noodles

¾ cup sour cream

2 tablespoons minced fresh parsley

Instructions

1. Season the meat with salt and pepper. Add the oil to the Instant Pot, and press Sauté. When hot, add the beef and cook for 3 minutes, or until evenly browned, working in batches as needed. Remove the browned meat from the Instant Pot and set aside.

2. Add the garlic, onion, mushrooms, and thyme to the pot. Cook for 3 minutes, stirring occasionally, or until tender.

3. Add the flour and whisk for 1 to 2 minutes, or until browned, then add the broth, sherry, Worcestershire sauce, mustard, paprika, and pepper; return the beef to the pot and stir.

4. Lock the lid and make sure the valve is sealed. Select Manual/High Pressure and adjust the time to 12 minutes.

5. When the cook time is complete, turn off the Instant Pot and let the pressure release naturally for 5 to 10 minutes before turning the valve to venting. Then, remove the lid.

6. Stir in the egg noodles. Lock the lid again, select Manual/High Pressure, and adjust the time to 5 minutes. When the cook time is complete, manually release the pressure.

7. Stir in the sour cream, and top with the parsley before serving.

Instant Pot Gumbo

The official state dish of Louisiana, gumbo can be made many different ways. This recipe creates a dark roux in the Instant Pot and is loaded with andouille sausage, chicken, and shrimp with a kick of Creole spice.

Makes 6–8 servings

Ingredients

2 tablespoons olive oil
1 red bell pepper, seeded and diced
1 green bell pepper, seeded and diced
1 onion, diced
2 celery ribs, chopped
3 cloves garlic, minced
2½ cups sliced andouille sausage
⅓ cup unsalted butter
⅓ cup all-purpose flour
3 cups Basic Chicken Bone Broth (page 41)
1 pound boneless, skinless chicken breasts, cut into 1-inch pieces
2 teaspoons Creole seasoning
1 (10-ounce) can tomatoes with green chiles
1 (14-ounce) can fire-roasted diced tomatoes
2 bay leaves
Salt and pepper, to taste
1 cup sliced okra
1 pound shrimp, peeled and deveined
4 cups cooked rice
Sliced green onions, for garnish

Instructions

1. Add the oil to the Instant Pot, and press Sauté. When hot, add the peppers, onion, celery, garlic, and sausage. Cook for 3 minutes, or until the vegetables are softened. Remove the vegetables and sausage from the pot and set aside.
2. Add the butter to the pot and stir. When the butter is melted, mix in the flour and cook for 5 minutes, stirring, until a roux is formed.
3. Add the broth, cooked vegetables and sausage, chicken, Creole seasoning, tomatoes, bay leaves, salt, and pepper.
4. Lock the lid and make sure the valve is sealed. Select Manual/High Pressure and adjust the time to 20 minutes.

5. When the cook time is complete, turn off the Instant Pot and let the pressure release naturally for 5 to 10 minutes before turning the valve to venting.

6. Remove the lid and add the okra. Press Sauté and cook, uncovered, for 5 minutes. Add the shrimp and cook for 5 more minutes, or until the shrimp are cooked through.

7. Discard the bay leaves, and serve over the rice topped with green onions.

Salmon with Kale

This simple salmon meal also works great with chopped bok choy or spinach. A neutral bone broth such as the Basic Chicken Bone Broth is best because you don't want it to overwhelm the dish.

Makes 4 servings

Ingredients
2 cups Basic Chicken Bone Broth (page 41)
2 tablespoons grated ginger
2 cloves garlic, minced
1 teaspoon plain rice vinegar
1 bunch kale, chopped into 1-inch slices
4 salmon fillets
Salt and pepper, to taste
¼ cup chopped green onions, for garnish

Instructions
1. Stir together the broth, ginger, garlic, and vinegar in the Instant Pot. Add the kale and stir.
2. Place the steaming rack in the Instant Pot over the kale. Place the salmon on the rack, skin-side down.
3. Lock the lid and make sure the valve is sealed. Select Manual/High Pressure and adjust the time to 4 minutes.
4. When the cook time is complete, turn off the Instant Pot and release the pressure manually. Then, remove the lid.
5. Remove the salmon with a spatula and place on dinner plates. Then, carefully lift the rack out with an oven mitt. Remove the kale with a slotted spoon and arrange around the salmon. Season with salt and pepper and top with the green onions.

Shepherd's Pie

Using the Instant Pot saves tons of time and energy in making this family favorite. You can sneak in bone broth in two ways—pure bone broth swapped for standard broth and then Bone Broth Mashed Potatoes for another helping.

Makes 4 servings

Ingredients

2 tablespoons olive oil

1 pound ground beef or lamb

1½ cups Basic Beef Bone
   Broth (page 39)

1 tablespoon all-purpose flour

1 tablespoon Worcestershire sauce

1 teaspoon dried thyme

1 teaspoon garlic powder

1 teaspoon onion powder

Salt and pepper, to taste

2 carrots, peeled and diced

1 cup frozen peas

2 cups Bone Broth Mashed Potatoes
   (page 153)

1 tablespoon unsalted butter

Instructions

1. Add the oil to the Instant Pot, and press Sauté. When hot, add the ground beef and cook until no longer pink. Drain and return the beef to the pot.
2. Stir in the broth, flour, Worcestershire sauce, thyme, garlic powder, onion powder, salt, and pepper. Stir until the gravy begins bubbling and thickening. Turn off the Instant Pot.
3. Stir in the carrots and peas. Top with the prepared mashed potatoes and butter. Select Manual/Low Pressure and cook for 5 to 10 minutes, or until the vegetables are tender.
4. When the cook time is complete, turn off the Instant Pot and let the pressure release naturally for 5 minutes before turning the valve to venting. Then, remove the lid and serve.

Smoked Paprika Chicken with Chickpeas

Smoked paprika gives dishes a hearty, barbecue taste that goes great with chicken as well as chickpeas. Add some diced potatoes and extra bone broth if you want more of a stew. Either way, served with a side salad, it's a complete meal for a weeknight dinner in less than 20 minutes.

Makes 4 servings

Ingredients

1 tablespoon olive oil

1 medium onion, chopped

1 pound chicken legs, thighs, or breasts

1 cup Basic Chicken Bone Broth (page 41)

2 cloves garlic, minced

2 tablespoons smoked paprika

Salt and pepper, to taste

¼ teaspoon ground coriander

1 (15.5-ounce) can chickpeas, drained and rinsed

Freshly chopped parsley, for garnish

Instructions

1. Add the oil to the Instant Pot, and press Sauté. When hot, add the onion and cook for 3 minutes, or until translucent.
2. Add the chicken and cook for 5 minutes, stirring frequently.
3. Add the broth, garlic, paprika, salt, pepper, coriander, and chickpeas; stir.
4. Lock the lid and make sure the valve is sealed. Select Manual/High Pressure and adjust the time to 6 minutes.
5. When the cook time is complete, turn off the Instant Pot and let the pressure release naturally for 5 minutes before turning the valve to venting. Then, remove the lid. Serve topped with parsley.

Chicken & Mushroom Risotto

There's no need to slave over the stove to make an authentic-tasting Italian risotto! This version cooks up so creamy with bone broth in your Instant Pot. Experiment with adding other veggies, such as asparagus, artichokes, zucchini, or peas.

Makes 4 servings

Ingredients

2 tablespoons olive oil, divided

1 onion, chopped

8 ounces cremini mushrooms, sliced

3 cloves garlic, minced

1 tablespoon chopped fresh thyme leaves

1 teaspoon salt, plus more to taste

2 teaspoons dried rosemary

3 teaspoons dried oregano

2 teaspoons paprika

¼ teaspoon pepper, plus more to taste

1 pound boneless, skinless chicken breast, cut into 1-inch pieces

4 cups Basic Chicken Bone Broth (page 41)

2 cups short-grain rice, rinsed

3 tablespoons unsalted butter

¾ cup grated Parmesan cheese

Instructions

1. Add 1 tablespoon of the oil to the Instant Pot, and press Sauté. When hot, add the onion and cook for 3 minutes, or until translucent.
2. Add the mushrooms, garlic, and thyme, and cook for 5 minutes. Remove the mixture from the pot and set aside.
3. Combine the salt, rosemary, oregano, paprika, and pepper in a small bow. Season the chicken with the mixture.
4. Add the remaining 1 tablespoon olive oil to the pot, and press Sauté. When hot, add the chicken and cook for 3 minutes, or until evenly browned.
5. Add the mushroom mixture back to the pot. Add the broth and rice; stir.
6. Lock the lid and make sure the valve is sealed. Select Manual/High Pressure and adjust the time to 4 minutes.
7. When the cook time is complete, turn off the Instant Pot and let the pressure release naturally for 5 to 10 minutes before turning the valve to venting. Then, remove the lid.
8. Stir in the butter and Parmesan.

Instant Pot Roast

This recipe makes for an unbelievably tender and flavorful roast that the whole family will love. For an outstanding meal that offers bonus bone broth, serve with Bone Broth Mashed Potatoes (page 153) and Braised Carrots & Kale (page 145).

Makes 8 servings

Ingredients
4 pounds boneless chuck roast
Salt and pepper, to taste
1 tablespoon olive oil
1 cup Basic Beef Bone Broth (page 39)
2 onions, quartered
2 celery ribs, chopped
2 carrots, peeled and chopped
2 bay leaves
2 cloves garlic, minced
¼ cup cold water
2 tablespoons cornstarch

Instructions
1. Season the roast with salt and pepper. Add the oil to the Instant Pot, and press Sauté. When hot, add the roast and sear for 2 to 3 minutes on both sides.
2. Add the broth. Place the onions, celery, carrots, bay leaves, and garlic over the roast.
3. Lock the lid and make sure the valve is sealed. Select Manual/High Pressure and adjust the time to 50 minutes.
4. When the cook time is complete, turn off the Instant Pot and let the pressure release naturally for 5 to 10 minutes before turning the valve to venting. Then, remove the lid.
5. Remove the roast and place on a plate. Use a slotted spoon to keep the liquid in the pot but remove and discard the vegetables.
6. In a small bowl, mix together the water and cornstarch until you have a slurry.
7. Add the slurry to the liquid remaining in the pot and stir. Press Sauté, and bring it to a simmer, stirring often until the gravy reaches the desired consistency. Place the gravy in a boat, and serve with the roast.

Curry Chicken with Sweet Potatoes

Sweet yet not lacking in kick, this super-quick entrée creates a wonderful curry sauce as the sweet potatoes dissolve into it. In less than 30 minutes, it's ready to hit your dinner table! Serve alone or over rice.

Makes 4 servings

Ingredients

1 tablespoon olive oil

1 small onion, diced

3 cloves garlic, minced

1 pound boneless, skinless chicken breast, cut into 1-inch pieces

1 sweet potato, peeled and cut into 1-inch cubes

1 red bell pepper, seeded and diced

1 green bell pepper, seeded and diced

1 cup green beans

1 cup Basic Chicken Bone Broth (page 41)

3 tablespoons curry powder

1 teaspoon ground cumin

1 teaspoon turmeric

1 (14-ounce) can coconut milk

Chopped fresh cilantro, for garnish

Instructions

1. Add the oil to the Instant Pot, and press Sauté. When hot, add the onion and garlic and cook for 3 minutes, or until the onion is translucent.
2. Add the chicken, sweet potato, peppers, green beans, broth, curry powder, cumin, and turmeric.
3. Lock the lid and make sure the valve is sealed. Select Manual/High Pressure and adjust the time to 12 minutes.
4. When the cook time is complete, turn off the Instant Pot and let the pressure release naturally for 5 to 10 minutes before turning the valve to venting. Then, remove the lid.
5. Return to Sauté and stir in the coconut milk. Simmer until warm. Garnish with the cilantro before serving.

Pulled Pork

While traditionally pulled pork is slow smoked over wood for several hours, you don't have to tell anyone it only took 90 minutes in the Instant Pot. Share the delicious results made with bone broth—but maybe not your cooking secret!

Makes 8 servings

Ingredients
1 tablespoon onion powder
1 tablespoon garlic powder
1 tablespoon smoked paprika
1 tablespoon red chili powder
1 tablespoon ground cumin
Salt and pepper, to taste
4 pounds bone-in or boneless pork shoulder
2 cups Basic Chicken Bone Broth (page 41)
2–3 cups barbecue sauce of your choice*
8 buns, for serving
Sliced red cabbage, for topping
Pickles, for topping

TIP
For a great homemade barbecue sauce, whisk together in a medium bowl 1½ cups ketchup, ¾ cup apple cider vinegar, ½ cup Dijon mustard, 2 tablespoons Worcestershire sauce, and ¼ cup brown sugar.

Instructions
1. Mix together the onion powder, garlic powder, smoked paprika, red chili powder, cumin, salt, and pepper in a small bowl. Rub the pork with the seasoning mixture.
2. Add the pork and broth to the Instant Pot. Lock the lid and make sure the valve is sealed. Select Manual/High Pressure and adjust the time to 90 minutes.
3. When the cook time is complete, turn off the Instant Pot and let the pressure release naturally for 5 to 10 minutes before turning the valve to venting. Then, remove the lid and place the pork in a large bowl.
4. Shred the pork with two forks. Remove the bones, if bone-in. Add the barbecue sauce and stir to coat.
5. Serve on the buns with cabbage, pickles, and a drizzle of barbecue sauce.

Chicken Cacciatore

This rustic Italian chicken dish is made so much simpler utilizing an Instant Pot. And you'll love the chicken, which will be so tender it will nearly fall apart on your fork. Serve over rice or noodles or with potatoes.

Makes 4 servings

Ingredients

2 pounds chicken breasts or thighs

Salt and pepper, to taste

2 tablespoons olive oil, plus more as needed

1 onion, diced

3 cloves garlic, minced

1 green bell pepper, seeded and diced

1 (14-ounce) can diced tomatoes

1½ cups sliced mushrooms

1 cup Basic Chicken Bone Broth (page 41)

¼ cup red wine vinegar

3 tablespoons tomato paste

1 teaspoon dried oregano

1 teaspoon paprika

1 teaspoon dried rosemary

1 teaspoon dried thyme

Fresh basil leaves, for garnish (optional)

Olives, for garnish (optional)

Instructions

1. Season the chicken pieces with salt and pepper. Add the oil to the Instant Pot, and press Sauté. When hot, add the chicken and cook for 3 minutes, or until evenly browned. Remove the chicken and set aside.
2. Add more oil to the pot if needed. Add the onion, garlic, and bell pepper and cook for 3 minutes, or until the onion is translucent.
3. Stir in the chicken, tomatoes, mushrooms, broth, vinegar, tomato paste, oregano, paprika, rosemary, and thyme. Lock the lid and make sure the valve is sealed. Select Manual/High Pressure and adjust the time to 10 minutes.
4. When the cook time is complete, turn off the Instant Pot and let the pressure release naturally for 5 to 10 minutes before turning the valve to venting. Then, remove the lid.
5. Top with basil leaves and olives if desired.

Chicken Marsala

This recipe calls for marsala wine, which is often used to create rich sauces. You can substitute a dry white wine for the marsala if you wish. Or, if you don't want to use any alcohol, simply add the same amount of broth instead. The dish is delicious serves with Bone Broth Mashed Potatoes (page 153) or over pasta or rice.

Makes 4 servings

Ingredients

4 large chicken thighs or breasts

Salt and pepper, to taste

½ cup all-purpose flour

2 tablespoons olive oil, plus more
   if needed

8 ounces fresh cremini mushrooms,
   thickly sliced

3 green onions, chopped

2 cloves garlic, minced

1 cup Basic Chicken Bone Broth
   (page 41)

⅓ cup marsala wine

⅓ cup heavy cream

Chopped fresh parsley, for garnish

Instructions

1. Season the chicken with salt and pepper. Place the flour on a plate and dredge the chicken in the flour on all sides.
2. Add the oil to the Instant Pot, and press Sauté. When hot, add the chicken and cook for 3 minutes, or until evenly browned. Remove the chicken from the pot and set aside.
3. Add more oil to the pot if needed and stir in the mushrooms, green onions, and garlic. Cook for 3 minutes.
4. Stir in the broth and return the chicken to the pot. Lock the lid and make sure the valve is sealed. Select Manual/High Pressure and adjust the time to 10 minutes.
5. When the cook time is complete, turn off the Instant Pot and let the pressure release naturally for 5 to 10 minutes before turning the valve to venting. Then, remove the lid.
6. Place the chicken on a plate. Return the pot to Sauté and stir in the wine. Bring the wine to a boil for 3 minutes. Stir in the cream and cook for 5 minutes, or until the mixture is thickened. Pour the sauce over the chicken, and garnish with the parsley.

Italian Meatballs

These tender meatballs will taste as if they have been simmering in a pot of sauce all day—the authentic Italian way. But all you really need is your Instant Pot to do the work in minutes. Serve the meatballs topped with Bone Broth Pasta Sauce (page 151).

Makes 6–8 servings

Ingredients

1 tablespoon olive oil

3 cloves garlic, minced

1 small onion, minced

1½ cups bread crumbs

4 cups Basic Beef Bone Broth (page 39), divided

1 pound ground beef

1½ pounds ground pork

¾ cup grated Parmesan cheese

1 teaspoon salt

½ teaspoon pepper

2 large eggs, beaten

Instructions

1. Add the oil to the Instant Pot, and press Sauté. When hot, add the garlic and onion. Cook for 3 minutes, or until the onion is translucent. Remove from the pot and set aside.
2. Meanwhile, in a small bowl, soak the bread crumbs in 2 cups of the broth.
3. Add the beef, pork, Parmesan, salt, pepper, and eggs to the bread crumb mixture. Mix and form into 2-inch meatballs. Place in the Instant Pot.
4. Add the remaining 2 cups broth to the Instant Pot. Lock the lid and make sure the valve is sealed. Select Manual/High Pressure and adjust the time to 20 minutes.
5. When the cook time is complete, turn off the Instant Pot and let the pressure release naturally for 5 to 10 minutes before turning the valve to venting.
6. Remove the lid and lift the meatballs from the broth with a slotted spoon.

Conversion Charts

METRIC EQUIVALENT MEASUREMENTS

If you're accustomed to using metric measurements, I don't want you to be inconvenienced by the imperial measurements I use in this book.

Use this handy chart, too, to figure out the size of the slow cooker you'll need for each recipe.

Weight (Dry Ingredients)		
1 oz		30 g
4 oz	¼ lb	120 g
8 oz	½ lb	240 g
12 oz	¾ lb	360 g
16 oz	1 lb	480 g
32 oz	2 lb	960 g

Volume (Liquid Ingredients)		
½ tsp.		2 ml
1 tsp.		5 ml
1 Tbsp.	½ fl oz	15 ml
2 Tbsp.	1 fl oz	30 ml
¼ cup	2 fl oz	60 ml
⅓ cup	3 fl oz	80 ml
½ cup	4 fl oz	120 ml
⅔ cup	5 fl oz	160 ml
¾ cup	6 fl oz	180 ml
1 cup	8 fl oz	240 ml
1 pt	16 fl oz	480 ml
1 qt	32 fl oz	960 ml

Length	
¼ in	6 mm
½ in	13 mm
¾ in	19 mm
1 in	25 mm
6 in	15 cm
12 in	30 cm

Index